The Airgun Hunter's Year

*This book is dedicated to my Mum, Mary Anne Mawn,
who always believed that I would one day write a book
– though I don't think she anticipated waiting
40 years for it to happen!*

The Airgun Hunter's Year

From dawn to dusk throughout the seasons

IAN BARNETT

Merlin Unwin Books

First published in Great Britain by Merlin Unwin Books, 2011

Text © Ian Barnett, 2011

Merlin Unwin Books Ltd
Palmers House
7 Corve Street
Ludlow, Shropshire SY8 1DB
U.K.

www.merlinunwin.co.uk
email: books@merlinunwin.co.uk

ISBN 978-1-906122-28-7

Designed and set in Bembo by Pauline Sterckx
Printed and bound by Great Wall Printing, Hong Kong

Contents

Foreword

There are many books available that tell the air-rifle hunter the where-with-alls of identifying and shooting quarry. They will tell you which guns to use, the best kit to acquire, how to zero, the different hunting techniques, ammunition types, gun maintenance *et al.* Fine books they are, too, and I have every single one on my bookshelf. In nearly all of them, though, there is something missing for me as a reader. The missing link isn't combining the simple mechanics of air rifle hunting with the tricks, tips and field-craft of the skilled hunter. Some of the books do that. The absent factor for me, an avid country sports reader, is the countryside itself. Anyone who has read the passionate, descriptive works of the old country writers will grasp what I mean. The late 'BB' on wildfowling, Richard Jeffries on rural matters in a bygone time, Brian Plummer on lurchers and terriers, Ian Niall, Jones & Woodward... the list is long. Standing behind a gun and knowing how to shoot it is one thing. Understanding the natural world in front of the muzzle is another.

I need to make one thing clear. I am not an expert on airguns. I am not a technician. I am a hunter and it just so happens that the air rifle is my preferred tool. Those that I own, I know how to use well: the proof is in here for you to see.

Yet in a way this is also a 'how-to' book, just like those others, but you'll have to search the narrative a little deeper for all those dark secrets gleaned in a lifetime of hunting. They're in there, I promise. It's primarily about how one old airgunning hack enjoys the countryside around him and processes the fruits of his expeditions. It attempts to impart my own knowledge of vermin species and how to attend to them. It is mostly for the hunter, very rarely for the technician, but also for anyone who enjoys country sports.

Knowing the ways of bird and beast, knowing the habitat in which you hunt and understanding how factors such as weather and crop cycles affect both are key to success in the field. Set across a typical British year, with a few historical anecdotes thrown in, I hope my effort relays the drive to hunt which runs through my blood. If guns were banned tomorrow I would hunt with bow, spear, catapult or any means at my disposal. Take them all away and I would simply walk the fields with a stick and a camera. It's not the end result of the hunt that matters to me. It's the 'being out there', challenging both vermin and weather. It's the ambience of a day (or night) in that wonderful amphitheatre that is our birthright: the countryside.

This book is about such days and nights. If I can take you there, into that ambience, and you learn a little bit along the way, then I have done what I set out to do. To entertain and to share a little knowledge along the way.

Curriculum Vitae

I grew up on a council estate in Hertford-shire during the 1960s. I was a street urchin with a difference: I had a passion for nature. Those were times when parents let their kids roam with no fear of something menacing happening to them. All the scrapes I got into were of my own making. Living a mile from open country-side (which has long since disappeared under sprawling housing development) the woods, undulating crop fields, orchards and ponds were heaven for a ten-year-old. I spent every available moment with a troop of similarly-minded lads scrumping apples, fishing for minnows or newts and (I will confess) bird nesting. The latter was my preamble into 'hunting'. The rivalry to have the best egg collection in the gang was fierce. I always read ardently on all things countryside – and still do.

By the age of eleven I could classify almost every native British bird at a glance and knew what its egg looked like. I knew where they'd be likely to breed and had a penchant for finding their nests. Boys being boys, we soon had penknives (hidden from our parents) and whittled catapults or bows & arrows as hunting weapons.

My father, bless him, saw one of my first shabby attempts at a 'cattie' and laughed at it. He'd been brought up on the deprived back-streets of Cardiff in the 1930s and knew a little about self-survival. He stripped the feeble knicker elastic off

the catapult, then cut and fitted some strips of old bicycle inner tube.

Unbeknown to him, my father had just furnished me with a tool that would inspire a life-long obsession with hunting. It came with a warning. No killing anything (somewhat confusing from a man who bragged about his ability to hit a cat at 50 yards at my age) and no broken windows. It was confiscated and destroyed in front of me within weeks, when the window rule was breached during an over-enthusiastic practice session! It was too late though, as he'd now shown me how to make one!

The black market in weapons at playground level was indicative of the times: air pistols, knives, catapults – and I went to a Catholic school! Many of my schoolmates were the children of the Irish labourers who built the New Town in which we lived. Greyhounds, whippets, lurchers, ferrets, a little bit of poaching (*'Jest fur der pot, moind yer'*) were par for the course. One day I traded a transistor radio for an old Gat air pistol and a pocketful of pellets. About 12 years old and my first air gun! I couldn't wait to take it out to kill something. Anything. Thankfully it was totally ineffectual so nothing suffered as a result. I'd had better success with the cattie. It spent most of its life wrapped in a plastic bag and buried in a wood so that my Dad didn't know I had it and I could use it when I wanted.

A year on and I swapped it (plus a pair of binoculars) for an old Diana break-barrel spring gun in .177 calibre. My first

air-rifle! Too valuable (for a 13-year-old) to bury in a copse, this was hidden in my bedroom.

One day, when I was alone in the house, the lure of the starlings on a neighbour's roof overcame me.

I bagged five from the bedroom window during an afternoon and laid back on my bed to read. Later, I heard our neighbour calling for my Dad across the small picket fence when he'd got home from work. I peeped out of the window and they were both looking up at me. Tony, our neighbour, held a handful of dead starlings by their feet. The old man reached the bottom of the stairs before me, hands on hips. My bedroom was searched, the gun found and destroyed in front of my eyes. My father's anger and disappointment in me reduced him to tears, but now as a father myself I know he took the right course of action. Mind you, five starlings at 20 yards with an old springer was quite a feat!

Like many lads, my later teens were

more focussed on girls, music and alcohol: different hunting but no less challenging. In my early twenties I fell for the romance of the lurcher and its versatility. The hunting desire had kicked in again big-time and I spent a couple of years mooching around the farms and estates near me, poaching rabbits and hares.

The Knebworth grounds (more famous for pop concerts now) were heaven to me. The recollection of a game-keeper following me around a perimeter footpath in a Land Rover, waving a shotgun and challenging me to let Megan (my cross-collie lurcher) dare to cross his fence line shames me now. I can't believe I was so reckless. The only excuse I can offer is that I was young. Yet, I learned so much about hunting in those days: lamping, snaring, stalking, tracking, etc.

Then, life changed considerably. A sequence of personal events made me mature faster than I really wanted to and I went into 'career mode', worked hard for qualifications, stepped into a serious profession and inherited all the stress that goes with that.

During that period, I still spent every available moment 'in country', walking and studying wildlife, though rarely shooting. Twelve years ago I moved to Norfolk, to a new life and with a new wife. She knew my history and recognised that I needed more than just 'work' and that golf or a similar hobby just isn't my 'thing'. We sought out a lurcher pup and the hunting desire was revitalised yet again. Cheryl bought me a

BSA Lightning as a birthday present and for the first time in my life I realised I had a partner who understood my psyche. I was 41 then. Now, at 53 years old, I'm a legitimate and responsible airgun hunter and photographer. So I've been shooting air guns on and off for 40 years, I suppose, but it's only in the last 12 that I've appreciated their real value as a hunting tool.

Since then, I've always kept a photo-journal of my hunting. As I'd always read a number of shooting periodicals I sent a piece to James Marchington at *Sporting Shooter* about shooting a family of magpies off a cow's back. The story is featured in this book.

Subsequently, I got a call from Nigel Allen, then Publishing Editor of *Airgunner* magazine, who persuaded me that readers would enjoy regular features of this type and my 'Hunting Scrapbook' started. Over the ensuing years I wrote for *Shooting Times*, *The Countryman's Weekly* and *Sporting Rifle* too and still write for most today. I learnt a lot about wildlife and hunting through reading. If I can pass on a little bit more to my fellow enthusiasts, then I will have left a legacy.

I would advise anyone, young or old, to read anything they can get their hands on. Study your quarry intimately, know its habits, habitat, breeding cycles, kill-zones, tracks and spoor. If the fruit of a successful hunt is edible, know how to dress it and cook it.

Listen to all the advice you're given but ignore braggarts. Learn to get in close to your quarry, really close, for that is true hunting.

Despite all that reading, I have learnt far, far more about the art of air rifle hunting out there in the field. Now might that tempt many readers to close this book before they start it and pick up their gun?

I would say 'do it!' Come back when the rain is driving down or the fog has descended. Open a bottle of wine or pour a large whisky or boil the kettle. And join me then, for a year in the countryside with an air rifle.

January

Hunger

Through wood and field and ditch, a fierce wind blows
Ridden, in celebration, by the crows.
The magpies flock and mock the Hunter's form
As he trudges, wrapped in fleece against the storm.
He checks the empty traps and checks the snare
The food he yearns, he'll find he knows not where
He loads his gun and to Diana pleads
For the single coney for the pot, he needs.

Sanctuary and symphony

It may seem a little odd to open a book about air rifle hunting with a piece about shooting indoors. This winter has been unpredictable again and deprived of harsh rime and carpets of virgin snow we have been beset by squalls and hailstorms. How I've longed for an enduring cold snap and prolonged snowfall, the type of winter we used to enjoy, where icicles cling to the eaves and Mother Nature's deep freeze wipes the countryside clean, killing off disease, culling the weak of every species and setting out her stall for spring.

Instead, the farmland is a cloying, sticky mire. The winter crops have been beaten down by the torrent from above and lashed by gales. There is a miserable, grey dampness exuding from the landscape and the sun has been in hibernation for weeks. I yearn for a cold, clear sky above a hoar-hardened ground, twinkling beneath the full moon and waiting to be thawed gently by the morning sun. Until then, I shall try to look for vermin control in more comfortable surroundings than the dripping copse or fog-bound meadow, though I will still venture there from time to time.

The farmyard is always a fruitful hunting ground. Here there will always, through every season, be rich pickings for unwelcome vermin and more so in the depths of winter when spilled animal feed, stored grain and heaped root vegetables offer a vast dining table, to be plundered if unguarded. Even the warmth of the infra-structure will be welcomed by the chilled bird or beast. In most cases, while the theft of expensive livestock fodder is frustrating to the farmer, it is the threat of spoilage and disease which demands your presence as a pest controller.

Cattleshed rat and pigeon shooting

The brown rat, who quite happily spent its summer in its holiday home beneath a hedge or along the water course, has now dug in under the stacked hay bales and below the cattle pens. From here, it will not only enjoy shelter from the elements but it is within yards of its own local supermarket: and the food is remarkably cheap! When the rat goes shopping, it will mark its trail back and forth with a potentially lethal spray of urine, pleasant little chap that he is. The leptospires in this invisible deposit can transfer easily to livestock, dog or human causing infertility in the former but can be fatal to the two latter hosts.

Weil's Disease (in man or dog) is a dreadful, debilitating illness and rarely survived. The feral pigeon will have arrived to roost on the girders and eaves. It, too, enjoys the easy access to the grain silo. It, too, will contaminate the pile as it feeds. In one end and out of the other. Pigeon guano can contain E. coli, salmonella and other horrors. These, if fed to young livestock via the spoiled grain, can kill. If you know the value of a bullock, you will appreciate why the farmer doesn't welcome the risk the small pigeon or the rat poses to his herd. Of course, there are other vermin visiting the farmyard too but they are mainly just chancers and thieves.

Today I've called the farmer and asked if I can spend some time around the cattle pens. It's a wet, windy Sunday and I'm desperate to be out with the gun for a while. Yesterday was written-off, the gales too bad to consider shooting such a feeble missile as an airgun pellet with any expectation of accuracy. For the uninitiated, we air rifle hunters don't shoot at live quarry unless almost certain of a clean kill. Respect for quarry is paramount and shooting in a gale is pointless and unethical. The blow has receded but it's still not ideal.

Sunday is a great day to be around the farmyard. The farmhands, who work seven days a week during spring and summer, will be at home. The farmer will hopefully slip down to the local for a pint or two and take a well-deserved siesta on his return. I will have the run of the farm, with no disturbance and no safety risks, for a couple of hours. One of my hosts, knowing that I will be around for a few hours, takes the opportunity to bundle the family into the 4x4 and to go shopping, grab a Mac, catch a movie, whatever, without going through all the rigmarole of blocking or locking gates, securing machinery etc. Rural crime is a constant worry for farmers. Machinery and stock are valuable assets. When you next lock the front door of your home, imagine how difficult it is to secure a farm and abandon it, worry free, for a day?

So when I drive into the yard, all is quiet. I leave the Jeep up by the farmhouse. This serves two purposes. When he gets back, my farmer will know that I'm either still there, or gone! A simple safety warning. It also lets any prospective visitor, welcome or unwelcome, know that someone's here.

Indoor shooting kit

I need little kit today. In my bag I've got ammo, a tripod seat, gloves, hat, snood, bean-bag, a few secrets and a camera – always the camera. Though I often have an outing where I don't shoot anything, I never have an outing where I don't photograph something. With a light, freezing rain falling, I take the gun from its slip (for it will never travel undressed) load a magazine of pellets, cock it ready to fire, snap on the safety catch, lock the Jeep and set off down the hill to the pens. Within the first 20 steps – and I'm still 200 yards from them, out of sight – a horde of woodpigeons flee the muster yard where they have been picking at spilt grain.

In the trees beyond the huge cattle shed, the rooks are watching me, holding fast to the swaying ash boughs, flapping to discharge the raindrops from their wings and already cackling like gossiping fishwives. They will take to the air before I reach the sheds, screeching *'Gun, gun, gun!'* Or so it sounds. Just inside the nearby wood, I can hear the chatter of that most elusive enemy, the magpie. Will he fall for my tricks today? We will see. It's all quite amusing, really. I can't creep into position so I must walk brazenly to the sheds. They seem to know what I'm about, but I know their foibles too. It's going to be an interesting afternoon.

I slip quietly into the gloom of the huge shed, the size of a hockey pitch, keeping to the shadows. At one end, the huge machines that work this farm are parked and I steal behind their cover.

The huge cattle shed – sanctuary on a windy day

Preparing to shoot

For a few minutes I stop to let my eyes adjust. I know full well that some of my quarry are watching me already. Not a particular problem, as they are used to human presence. They won't associate me with malice just yet, but soon they will. Those that escape will remember. So, like some rural Ninja warrior, I'm darkly dressed and the snood is pulled up above my cheeks and nose. The peak of a baseball cap hides my eyes. I have warm shooting mittens on, which will prove to be crucial later. My weapon of choice is a legal limit (sub 12ft/lb) silenced, pre-charged, multi-shot air rifle. Sounds a mouthful doesn't it? A standard gun for an air rifle hunter. The pellet will hit its quarry with an impact of around 8ft/lb at 30 yards. The victim will probably have not heard it being discharged at that range. The power, though low compared to a rim-fire rifle or shotgun, is enough to crash through a rabbit's skull at 60 yards. Terminal power. These squatting targets, at the moment indifferent to my presence, will topple easily to an accurately placed shot. I'm not here to practice. I've done that, over many years, on thousands of inert objects and if I hadn't, I would have no right to be here. These little guys are in trouble.

The huddled forms on the girders in the roof range from about 15 to 35 yards away. Those sitting at 25 yards are ideal and through the scope I can distinguish head from body. I'm cautious of the backstops. The perspex skylights are fragile and must be avoided. The weather, unexpectedly, comes to my aid. The heavens open and the drumming on the aluminium roof resonates around this large auditorium like a class of kids sprinting along a gymnasium floor.

The first shot goes almost un-noticed but as the feral pigeon drops from its beam, its neighbours flutter off to the opposite end of the building, above the stock pens. Taking advantage of the noise, I pick off a couple more. A fourth expires, but remains on the beam. Damn! I'll deal with that later. All the time, the birds are playing musical chairs but some have wised-up and flashed off into the rain outside. Time for a break. I move down the shed and take cover near the pens, where most of the herd are in residence.

It's not a pleasant place but at least it's dry. If the beating of the rain on the roof was the percussion for today's strange concert then the cattle are the wind section. The next hour was spent listening to a symphony of belching, farting, squit-ting and urination. The rank odours of methane and ammonia pervaded, but above the rising fog of frozen breath, my targets were still sitting and the work continued. More caution was needed now.

Livestock: extra precautions called for

A deflected pellet would bounce harmlessly off thick hide but a ricochet in the eye of an £800 beast would be intolerable to a farmer. So each shot is carefully measured and mostly taken at birds above the centre aisle. I had no desire to recover dead birds from among these hulks, and clearing up after yourself is another 'must-do' for the shooter. The session ended with a fair score – eleven birds – and when the farmer arrived to feed the cattle, I departed gracefully.

Potting feral pigeons – useful winter work

Greed and consequence

A week later and with little improve-ment in the weather, I'm back at the barn. Not after ferals, particularly, but to use some tricks against a much more worthy opponent. The muster yard at the end of the building has been attracting a pirate crew – a magpie flock. I've had my beady eyes on this audacious gang, about 15 strong, for some weeks now. They dance and cackle around the roof (rarely venturing inside the shed) and they gather on the ash trees overlooking the yard. A few will play look-out while others dip down to steal grain and spilled oats. Previous approaches to the barn, on my own, have seen them screech off, alarmed. Sitting up at the wood's edge one morning, I noted that the activity of the farmhands didn't seem to worry them at all. How can these birds distinguish between one man's indifference and anoth-er's murderous design? It amazes me.

Baited magpies

Today I was in shed early, while the farm was active. I set out my box of tricks – a flock magpie decoy and a gutted rabbit – beneath the gate to the muster yard. I backed off and sat to wait for an hour, deep inside the building. Eventually the guys finished their work and headed off, leaving me alone in the shed. This is not a new ruse, by any means, and the old adage that 'crows can't count' is used often. It applies to pigeons too.

Before long, the magpie tribe, undoubtedly watching from afar for an opportunity and duped by the exit of the farmhands, rattled and chattered along the blackthorn hedges and into the elms. They were screaming alarm calls and threats at my decoy.

Deep in the shed...
scoping baited magpies

Gun and camera at the ready

Back in the shadows, I readied both gun and camera. Now, I reckon I'm quite adept with the gun. I've also got a reputa-tion for a fairly good photo. But I've never mastered the art of operating both at the same time! When the magpies started to flash across the open end of the shed, mobbing my decoy, I opted for the camera. Murphy's Law applied and while I had the viewfinder at my eye, one of the pies landed on the gate and another on the floor, harassing the fake bird. I switched to the rifle but too late. They'd flown again. Back to the camera – in they came again.

This frustrating sketch was repeated a few times and I finally set down the camera to concentrate on shooting the little beggars.

Placing decoys at a useful distance

Now, there was a bit of science in my placement of the decoy and rabbit. Beneath the gate, visible from the elms and exactly forty paces from my hideout, the length of the cattle pens. When one of the tribe hit the floor again to threaten my flock decoy, I knew it was just short of forty yards from my muzzle when it died.

Outside, all hell broke loose. The others buzzed and dived around the yard, distraught at the killing of a fellow bandit. The second victim was foolish enough to land on top of the gate. The same forty yards, sweetly placed for my zeroed scope and its graded mil-dots. The shot knocked it into the mud in the yard.

This time, instead of pandemonium, there was a stunned, almost spooky, silence. Then, a couple of harsh chatters and through the slats above the entrance I saw a black and white evacuation. One of them had called the retreat. I retrieved the dead birds but waited on for a while and the decoy scene attracted a passing crow, eager for the rabbit innards. This time, knowing the fickleness of the crow I let it sit on the gate, though it was a tempting target.

Only when it was confident enough to flap down to peck at the bait did I release the shot.

Some tolerance for the jackdaw

Later, a jackdaw did the same and I stole its soul with my camera lens rather than a pellet. I will shoot jackdaws when they are caught in the act, stealing grain, but unlike its cousins, this amusing and aerobatic corvid rarely attacks songbird nests or chicks so I will tolerate it up to a point. My mind was on the magpies. Two down,

Magpies often come to inspect a dead comrade

thirteen to go, in this gathering. The problem being the thirteen left, now with an education. Every one of them would be harder to get near next time.

That's why old *'pica pica'* is such a natural survivor, such a worthy adversary and why we have seen such an explosion in their numbers over recent years.

The magpies and the cow

A few winters ago, after posting out some of my 'free vermin control' cards to local farmers, I received a very strange phone call. The farmer, William, explained that he had an old cow, a favourite of his, with a worrying problem. She had developed an abscess on the base of her tail earlier in the year: an open wound. The vet had been applying lotions in an attempt to dry out and disinfect the wound but the treatment was being negated by the attentions of a particular pest which was keeping the abscess open and, worse still, aggravating it. William explained that a female magpie was gorging on the infected flesh.

Baby magpies learn quickly

Since the spring, she had introduced two of her youngsters to the feast. The tribe were eating the cow alive, attracted by the blood of the open wound. William and his kin had tried to catch the maggies using Larsen traps with no success. They avoided the shotgun and were very wary of human approach. I asked William how he thought I could help? He posed a very challenging question. Could I shoot the birds off the cow's back, as this was when they were most vulnerable? With a deep gulp of breath, I said yes, I could, if I could get near enough? I agreed to drive over and take a look on Saturday.

When I arrived, William identified the old cow. She was with her herd, gorging on kale in a nearby field. It was bitterly cold and threatening snow. As we watched through binoculars, the magpies floated in. The mother bird landed on her back, the younger birds perched in nearby bushes. She hopped down to the tail of the cow and started to feed. I couldn't believe what I was seeing. Shortly after, the two youngsters joined her. As they pecked, the old cow kept browsing and flicked her tail feebly trying to dislodge the birds, with no success. I asked William how often they were feeding. He looked glum and answered 'twenty, maybe thirty times a day!'

Agreed risk with the farmer

I noted a thin strip of copse close to the field and the fact that William was sectioning the kale fodder with electric wire. He agreed to contain the herd close to the copse, on the kale, using the wires on Sunday morning. We agreed a disclaimer: I would attempt the cull but wouldn't be held responsible for injury to the cow. We both agreed that the effect of a .22 pellet on the hide of an old cow was preferable to the ignominy she was enduring now.

At home that night, I wrestled with gun choice. A PCP would be silent and accurate but what if I missed and it took me all day? I could run out of air. Prior to that, the depleting air could cause power loss and I might hit the cow. PCP's are also temperature sensitive, and it was going to be cold out there tomorrow. I settled on my old BSA Lightning, a spring gun.

*The magpie was feasting
on the raw abscess*

consistent power, no air-source required.

On Sunday morning I loaded a pop-up hide and my rifle into the motor in a snow squall. By the time I set up in the copse, we had heavy snowfall. Marvellous! True to his word, William had driven the herd into a wired-off section of the kale. Through the snowflakes I had trouble identifying the problem cow among the thirty-strong herd. Then I saw a flash of black and white. A magpie landed on one of the beasts. It was her. I lined up and took a shot, missing over the top. The bird fled. Damn!

I waited for an hour for the bird to return. I was frozen stiff. The weather was worsening and we now had a blizzard. The cattle, who I thought were contained, abandoned the kale and moved back behind me to take shelter in the field on the lee side of the copse.

I kept watching the old cow for another hour from within the hide, my fingers numb and the cold creeping up through my boots. I was about to pack up when I caught that flash of wings again. This time I had a camera with me and photographed the spectacle. Soon after the mother landed, one of the youngsters joined her as she fed. What I witnessed was fascinating: the older bird pecking at the flesh and feeding the younger bird, which was at least six to nine months old by now.

One down, one to go

I wasn't here to play 'David Attenborough' though. The camera was set down and the gun raised. I waited for the mother bird to hop up onto the cow's spine again, to feed her offspring. Thirty-five yards, through falling snow. One of the best shots I've ever taken in my life with a spring gun. The older bird flopped into the mud; the youngster fled. The cow jinked but was unharmed.

The mother feeding its offspring

The end of an unusual assignment

Next generation challenge

A month later, William called again. The young magpies had inherited the taste for raw meat. They were helping themselves now, just as we had feared. I returned and finished the job in one session. With fairer weather and a PCP rifle, I shot one bird, then its sibling made the fatal mistake of fussing around the corpse. The cow's abscess repaired well but, sadly, old age caught up with her about a year ago. A strange story but one that reflects the versatility of the air rifle, I hope you agree.

The kitbag conundrum

You've got that gleaming new rifle, a pouch full of pellets and hours of target practise behind you. Now the prospect of hunting live quarry is tugging at you like a trawl net. You've got permission notes from landowners burning a hole in the pocket of your camouflage jacket and you're about to set out for the first time when you suddenly pause and think: *'What else will I need?'*

Blooded shooters will tell you that in the early years, after every hunt, they developed and built upon a wish-list, usually the consequence of frustration when they've thought: *'Damn, I wish I'd brought some nets!'* or *'Hell, I need some decoys!'*. It happens to all of us. Yet you just can't carry everything, all the time.

Even when targeting a specific quarry, the pure diversity of airgun hunting usually offers opportunities to shoot other quarry species. What's more, when you have planned to tackle a particular problem, Murphy's Law often kicks in.

For example, you've gone out with a small shoulder bag, gun and pellets to deal with a pair of magpies you keep seeing in the corner of a field. Two hours later you've got half a dozen rabbits but the magpies didn't show up. You didn't bring a knife because you don't paunch magpies, and nor did you bring a proper game-bag! You weren't going to bring the dead magpies home, were you? The two-mile hike back to your motor with six un-paunched, unhocked rabbits and a fairly heavy rifle will quickly teach you a lesson in simple logistics. Be prepared!

I learnt the hard way and now have a bare minimum of essentials that I carry, religiously, in my kitbag now. The kitbag itself is the result of years of searching for the right combination. The list of contents was gleaned through practical, and often

Game-bag and roe-sack

painful, experience. Yes, it makes for a slightly heavier load when I'm out for a hunting session but there are ways around this. All will be explained! So here's my inventory excluding my gun and ammo.

Two hunting bags

I carry two bags when hunting. The main one is a roe-sack. The name gives it away. These huge ruck-sack style bags are capable of carrying a gralloched (gutted) deer and

were designed for use by highland stalkers. Waterproof and with a washable inner liner, most also have a few pockets on the outside for ancillary kit.

Inside this I carry a smaller, more conventional game-bag. This has loads of compartments and pockets, plus outside net pouches. Inside this, too, are smaller bags for stowage and a fold-away bass bag which can carry up to about a dozen rabbits. The whole lot resembles one of those old Russian Dolls which some of you may recall – a doll within a doll within a doll. But why two main bags?

I like to have as much with me in the field as I can practically carry but remain stealthy. The roe-sack is carried into my hunting area and anything I think I *might* need as opposed to *definitely* need is held inside it, plus the smaller bag. I usually tuck this away under a hedge and withdraw the smaller bag, which carries everything I *definitely* need. So now, when I go walkabout, I'm carrying probably a third of the weight of the roe-sack but if I need anything from it, it's not too far away. Overleaf are lists of what I carry in each bag and you will see that in the smaller one, I always have the most important items around my shoulder.

The items listed overleaf may seem a lot but they will fit comfortably into the game bag – and remember, I even carry two cameras and a tripod in mine!

Right: The game-bag goes everywhere while hunting

Game-bag contents

My game-bag contents go everywhere on a hunt:

• A razor-sharp knife: an essential for paunching, hocking or trimming back light vegetation. Hunting without a knife is like fishing without a keep net. My Opinel No 7. is always close to hand.
• Permission notes and insurance details, carried in a BASC wallet. You may be challenged at any time and should be able to prove you are allowed where you are and that you are a responsible person. Not all your landowners staff will know you have a right to be present.
• Camo baseball cap and camo snood. I always wear a baseball cap to shield my eyes and hide my face from avian quarry. The lightweight snood keeps insects off my neck and covers my face when ambushing. In winter, these will be substituted for a fleece bob hat and fleece snood, plus gloves.
• Secateurs, for hides, trimming back twigs when shooting from cover and for game preparation in the field.
• Mini LED torch: summer, winter, night or day I carry one. Even a summer rabbit shot close to cover can flip (through nervous reaction) into the nearest hole. A quick check with the torch has added many rabbits to my bag when I first thought them lost.
• Lenspen: for the serious airgunner, your scope will be the second most expensive piece of kit you own (the first being the gun). Look after it.
Don't wipe the condensation on a cold evening or the detritus falling from the canopy when you're roost shooting with the corner of your coat! Use a proper cleaner like this.
• Mobile phone: an obvious essential but not just for emergencies. I always leave a card in my windscreen stating 'On land with permission' and showing my mobile number. Useful? I'll say. Varying from a text message saying *'Joint of beef in oil shed for you when you get back'*, to a phone call *'Can you get your arse back here and move your car. I can't get the baler through the gate, you muppet!'* And all this from the same farmer! Ho hum!
• Antiseptic hand wipes and disposable gloves because I often dress out quarry in the field. The stench of rabbit paunch is a lingering one and is even worse if you mistakenly puncture the gut. Do yourself a favour and keep hygiene in mind, particularly if you are a smoker or you eat and drink on the session. The gloves? You probably use them when you diesel-up your vehicle. And that's where I get them (wink, wink!)
• A bass-bag: a nylon net bag that rolls away and can be opened up to carry a bundle of rabbits or pigeons if I've been successful.
• Supermarket carrier bags: half a dozen, folded, take up no space and add no weight. Use them to wrap shot quarry and save yourself washing out the bass-bag. This will protect your other kit from bloodstains too. Fleas are a fact of life with rabbits and squir-

rels. Most will die in the bag instead of leaping all around your car on the trip home!

● Compact binoculars for long range observation, especially when pigeon decoying.

● Cameras and tripod – well they're obviously on my critical list, though not necessarily yours.

● Vermin calls are useful at times. Though I find, more and more, that fieldcraft and knowledge of quarry habits are far more effective.

● Pathfinder targets, for quick zero checks and often handy (when ambush shooting) to mark out distance with a visual aid. If you're bored, you can shoot them instead just to keep your eye in!

● Face net: camo, lightweight. Personally I hate wearing them but there are times when I tolerate it, such as crow or pigeon roost shooting. Mosquito territory being another.

● Hand-warmers in winter only. Most camping shops carry these little disposable powder packs. They are easily carried and can totally transform a hunting session on a freezing day. Warm fingers are more trigger sensitive and accurate. I wouldn't be without them in a cold snap.

● Scope covers popped on in bad weather to keep raindrops off the lenses.

● A spare air-cylinder – that makes one in both bags. Running out of air in a PCP rifle is a disaster when a hunt is going well.

The game-bag fits into the roe-sack

Roe-sack contents

The small game-bag.

● A roll-up rifle slip in case the weather turns foul.

● A tripod seat and small camo net in case I spot a good ambushing point.

● A drink bottle or hot flask (and sometimes food).

● A spare rifle air-cylinder (the Weihrauch ones are small).

● A tin of pellets.

● Some folded supermarket carrier bags to wrap bloody quarry.

● A micro fleece top, fleece bob-hat and gloves as cold weather protection.

● A spinner target in case I need to zero in the field.

● A spare knife in case I lose the other.

● A fold up saw for hide building.

● Insect repellent in summer, a spray can save a lot of discomfort. Seasonally, perhaps some pigeon decoy shells or magpie decoys.

● My Ledray lamping kit, to extend the hunting day, is often there too.

February

Tracking

The icy wood is still, in field no sound
Except the crunch of boot on hoary ground.
The Hunter's breath blows warmth into his hands
As once again he scans the frost-strewn lands.
In frozen track and trail, he reads the spoor
Like photographs etched into rimey floor.
And where they lead, though now it may not suit
In warmer days will bear a heavy fruit.

Forensic Fieldcraft

February is possibly the most barren month of the year for air rifle hunting. Short days and dire weather make can conspire to offer scarce opportunity. Yet it is, during a normal winter, a fine month to take stock of your shooting area and really learn about the presence of bird and beast on your land.

Come rain, hail, frost or snow, I will still be out and about with dog and gun. While I enjoy reading and writing for a spell, I tend to go 'stir-crazy' if confined within four walls for too long. For me, the hunting gene demands action as much as knowledge. I will happily wander from wood to way-mark, from field to farm, just exploring the land around me and becoming intimate with it. The true hunter is (by necessity) a mixture of naturalist, ornithologist, entomologist and crime-scene investigator.

To know and understand how to interpret each track, trail and sign will help to make the indifferent air-rifle hunter into an adept one.

Practical tracking

Forget all that old 'Lone Ranger' nonsense: 'three horses passed this way two weeks ago, Kemo Sabe. One ridden by a dwarf, another by a one-legged woman'. Reading animal and bird sign is fairly simple if you apply yourself and really want to learn it. Knowing the inhabitants of your land; their feeding habits, paths, dens, nest sites and roosts will add greatly to your chance of success in finding and controlling vermin.

So why February for this research? In truth, any winter month can be good. Wet days followed by a cold snap, especially hard frost or snow, are ideal times to study tracks

Snow provides the airgun hunter with an excellent tracking opportunity

Interpreting the signs

Often there is a story told in the trail. The rabbit tracks crossing those of the fox. The disturbance in the snow. The single tracks of the fox leading away – and the splatter of crimson which punctuates the trail. Old Charlie must have eaten well last night, having caught his quarry and carried his catch from the scene.

Prints of a fox pouncing on quarry

and trails. Around field gates, on muddy rides and alongside watercourses or pools you will find an abundance of footprints at the best of times. A frost will harden the previously soft ground and capture these tracks like a photograph, allowing close examination. In snow, fresh spoor will lead you to quarry or to its home.

During snowfall I have found rabbit warrens and rat lairs that I didn't know existed, simply by following tracks back to hedgerow and copse. I enjoy the challenge of reading animal and bird sign, trying to work out what a creature was doing, where it was going.

That's what adds an edge to tracking: working out what's going on when you're not around to witness it.

Reading sign isn't just about footprints, though. Feeding sign is common and can tell me where best to ambush vermin. The broken hazelnut kernels or beech-mast on the tree stump show a squirrel's dining table, well worth a watch with a gun at hand. The gnawed winter barley stalks tell me that two species of agricultural pest are at work here. The stepped height of the damage shows that rabbits have been plundering at low level but fallow deer have been browsing at the higher level. I can tackle the rabbits with my air rifle but the deer are the stalker's task. The trail of spilt grain along the barn floor tells me the rats have young in the nest already and, more importantly, where the nest is.

From a purely observational point of view, I always check the pile of pigeon feathers on the floor. Strewn in a circle, with the feather stems indented indicating the pull of a sharp bill, speaks of the sparrowhawk kill. Similarly, a carcase

Signs of a fox kill. A sparrowhawk would have cast the feathers more widely

with the breast stripped out will be the sparrowhawk too.

Watch this little hunter when you see her, for she will lead you directly to the pigeon roost, bombing her prey from the ivy in spectacular fashion.

A rough pile of feathers, with the stems scythed through, is vulpine work and it always amazes me that a fox can pounce on a normally wily woodpigeon. Now that would have been a stalk worth watching!

Animal spraints

There is another sign to examine carefully, though the task is less pleasant. Animal and bird droppings tell you much about a creature. Not just where it is feeding (and on what) but also its state of health. If the fox scat on a tussock is greyish, matted with fur, it is feeding well and there are rabbit

Fox stool on a stump – it's not eating well!

warrens close by. Move with his stealth and you, too, can expect rabbits in your bag. If those scats are dark, loose and full of shells the fox has fallen on hard times. The warrens are barren or it is injured, so he is feeding on worms and beetles. His coat will be poor and his general health lacking.

Similarly, green scats dotted with small bone show a fox reduced to a vegetarian diet supplemented with mice and voles. Your warrens aren't supplying him: are they empty, or is he sick?

The large patch of woodpigeon guano on the floor of the spinney will reveal the evening roost and should be memorised. You will note the 'layers' which indicate that this is a regular roost. A twilight sortie to catch them flighting-in should put meat in the freezer. Visit occasionally, not repeatedly, and you have a harvest point. Succulent medallions of pigeon breast to fill a pie, supplement a casserole or skewer on the summer barbeque. More on that later!

Rabbit and rat droppings are fairly obvious sign but look again. How fresh are they? What time of day is it? These clues will tell you when to lie in wait, for your quarry is a creature of habit and habit is the greatest chink in its armour. Just as you will return to a favourite restaurant time and time again, so will your quarry. During winter, hunger will often over-ride caution. So your quarry is vulnerable. Is that a moral problem? Remember, for most of the year, your quarry have the advantage of cover. Usually in crops. Now they don't. Use the opportunity and don't feel guilty.

Where there are rabbits...

Other mammal prints will point toward a rich harvest for the pot-filler. Badger, stoat and weasel won't stay long on land without rabbits. Their quarry is your quarry too. Welcome the tracks, but if with a gun in hand you spot the stoat or weasel, don't hesitate to cull them especially if your landowner shoots game. Though rarely seen, and entertaining to watch, these little mustelids are vicious and highly efficient assassins. If you've ever watched a stoat track and kill a rabbit, as I have, your admiration will make it hard to squeeze the trigger – until you imagine that the rabbit could be the hand-reared poult or the farmer's hen.

Bird pellets

Bird pellets are worth studying too. These are the disgorged contents of the stomach and are common to most avian pest species. Not only do they reveal the bird's diet but where they were found is worth remembering. Habit! Rooks, crows and jackdaws often disgorge on a regular post or stump, making them vulnerable to the hunter.

Dismantle the pellets with a twig and you'll learn much about their diet. Barley ears, earthworm and beetle carapace in the rooks pellet make it seem fairly innocuous as a pest in summer. The small bones and tiny shards of a fledgling's beak in spring

Rook pellet on a fencepost

tell you the real truth though, that even the rook won't overlook a vulnerable nest. It's a crow thing.

The magpie's pellet, rarely found except underneath the nest, will always give enough evidence to convict and guarantee the death penalty. Egg shell, bones, tiny claws, though in autumn it will be full of the wings and carapace of crane flies. When the 'daddy-long-legs' hatch out through the September meadow grass, old Pica will be dancing about like the bride's father at a wedding reception, trying to catch these gangly insects.

Bird pellets also tell you which raptors are present on your land. Admittedly you can't shoot the raptors and why would you want to? There are too few about nowadays, for my liking. Yet their mere existence on your land speaks of a healthy diversity and an availability of food. Much of their food is your quarry (rabbits, rats, mustelids) but some are not (voles, mice, shrews). Would you deny the hungry buzzard one of your target rabbits? I wouldn't, nor would I resent the sparrowhawk its expertly snatched woodpigeon. Around the bird-table or poult pens though? That's where they become unpopular but surely we must forgive them.

They, too, are hunters preying on the vulnerable, just like we are.

Evidence of corvid work – note the indent made by a beak

Eggshell clues

Later, in the spring, broken eggshells on the woodland floor, of woodpigeon, black-bird or thrushes eggs, bear closer examination. Long chinks match the harsh bill of a plundering magpie which will demand my attention.

If the shell is topped like my break-fast egg, the squirrels have been raiding. The cleanly halved shell tells me to look up, where the hatched pigeon squab sits fattening in its nest. Nothing sinister there.

Walking the land with my gun, I always have one eye on these matters. Spotting such sign is an important factor in my success with the air rifle. It's forensic science, hunters' style.

Permission to shoot, Sir?

The subject of difficulty in acquiring permission to shoot on private land is one that crops up in shooting circles time and time again. Just reflect on it. If a total stranger knocked your door and asked if they could play in your back garden from time to time, how would you react? That's exactly what you're doing when you approach a farmer or landowner for permission. Add to that your request to creep around their land with a weapon capable of wounding (or worse) farmhands or livestock. You have to understand why permission is sometimes just a tad difficult to come by!

I've only been living in East Anglia for around twelve years. When I first went in search of the Golden Fleece that we shooters call 'permission' I expected it to be difficult, particularly as my indigenous work colleagues warned me that the local farmers were feisty, insular and very wary of 'outsiders'. What a lot of nonsense that proved to be. In all this time I have only ever had one aggressive rejection, and that was from a lady who loves fluffy little bunnies even though they ravage her gardens and plunder her neighbour's crops. Indeed, her gardener has to sneak a mole controller in when she's away for a weekend! Many approaches to landowners were politely ignored but others bore fruit.

I now shoot around 5000 acres of excellent arable and wooded land and all of the landowners are amiable, approachable and co-operative.

The very first farm I gained here followed an enjoyable 'interview' and guided tour of the boundaries by the farmer. There was an embarrassing moment when my lurcher pup followed his older collie-cross bitch through a barbed wire fence. The pup punctured his flank and by the time we got back to my car it had opened up into two inch gash, bleeding heavily. I think Oliver, the farmer, felt sorry for us – and sent me away with a signed permission note which more than compensated

A quality business card will get you noticed

for the vet's bill I was given an hour later! But the call for an 'interview' was not an accident. It was the fruit harvested from intensive cultivation months earlier. I had used a simple 'sales' campaign.

First things first

Before I explain that, don't even think about using your air rifle on someone else's land (or your own, for that matter) without first buying public liability insurance. BASA, BASC or NGO membership will give you insurance cover and legal representation for just a few pence a day, the price of a few pellets.

As for the land search, I started with Ordnance Survey maps. I checked out the farm names, drove around looking at the type of agriculture and noted all those I wanted to contact. I then used a Royal Mail Postal Address Book to get the postcodes. Where possible, I found out the farmer's names. Next I put together a postcard (using Microsoft Publisher) to advertise free vermin control services.

My calling card

The card was important. It had to have visual impact and enough information to show a responsible approach. It had to show I was insured and how to contact me. I then sent a polite approach letter and a copy of the card to all the farms. Then I sat back and waited... and waited... and waited. Nothing. A month later, I sent it again. I also started to place the card around local nurseries, garden centres and

pet-food suppliers – places where country folk and farmers go.

Just when I thought I may have to change my tactics, I got three phone calls in a week. The first was not from a farmer, but from his daughter who lived on different land. She wanted her horse paddocks cleared. The horses were turning fetlocks in rabbit holes. The second was from Oliver, who invited me over for a chat. The third was from an elderly gent who wanted pigeons cleared from his huge garden.

I was off and away. Further land came from referrals and through simply tapping the knowledge of each landowner. Farmers network well: they have to. And there isn't anything happening locally that escapes their attention.

Introductory visit

So having got the call, what happens next? First, you arrange to visit. Dress country-casual (not full camo yet, save that for later!) but make sure you're equipped for a tour. Take your boots, rainwear etc. Don't take a dog unless it has been agreed with the landowner. If you do, take a leash and a bag to clear up in case it fouls the farmyard. Most farmers won't care but they will appreciate your respect for their 'garden'. Take, and show, proof of liability insurance.

By all means take a gun, suitably covered, in case the farmer wants to see it. They might, as happened to me once, ask you demonstrate your accuracy. I had to shoot a small potato, stuck on a fence post 40 yards away: one of the most pressured shots I have ever taken. The farmer (without the benefit of the view through my riflescope) grunted, nodding toward the potato which was intact on the fence and said 'You missed, boy!' I walked him over to the vegetable and showed him the tiny hole drilled through the middle. I got my permission.

So, make sure your rifle is zeroed. Remember, if you can't achieve a shot like that, confidently, you shouldn't be there. Other landowners have simply been fascinated to see the guns I use now and, watching them fired, surprised at the low volume. Hence the subscript on my cards. Air rifle pest control is discreet.

What to ask

Ask lots of questions. Not just about your own interests, which will be: what quarry is permitted and which boundaries prevail? Ask about family: are there children around? Any neighbours to upset? Public footpaths? What stock do they keep? Are there farm dogs, chickens, ducks, cats? (Many farms have 'mousers' prowling the yards). Talk about crops and crop rotation. Planting times? Harvesting? Access times? Do you need to phone before visiting? Can you lamp at night? Can you shoot around the farm buildings at suitable times? Make sure you are very clear on what species can be culled. One of my farmers, thankfully, told me he enjoys watching the jackdaws around his yard, so I let them be. Others

have asked me not to touch wild game-birds or hares, which are not really air rifle quarry anyway. Don't take anything for granted.

Carry out a risk-assessment

The visit is also a two-way exchange. As a responsible shooter, this is also your chance to carry out a risk-assessment. Never be afraid to decline land if you think it unsuitable. The elderly gent I mentioned earlier? His huge garden was urban and surrounded on two sides by houses and at the far end was a school. Shooting his nuisance pigeons would prove too risky, but I did recommend he place a plastic falcon decoy at one end of the garden, which quite tickled him. I even showed him where to get one. Now he gets mobbed by rooks instead! That, I can assure you, is not the only land I've declined. I stopped shooting rabbits on one wonderful farm simply because the farmer (a lonely old chap, I grant) took to following me about. It's difficult to stalk rabbits successfully when a 4x4 keeps screaming up and a head pops out to ask you how you're doing!

Get written permission

If all goes well and permission is agreed, discuss your need for a written permission note. Take it with you, typed and ready for a signature. This is very important nowadays and protects both parties. Study the current General Licenses issued by Natural England. Be sure you can explain to anyone in authority (police,

Leave your mobile number on display in you vehicle

How to please the landowner

So. Now you've got some permission. How do you make sure you keep it? The main rule is to visit regularly. If you don't, someone more keen will usurp your rights. Show the landowner that you are getting results. Remember to offer the odd rabbit or pigeon for the table.

Always stop and spare time for a chat with the farmer, landowner or their workers. Many will work all day without seeing another soul, so they will appreciate a yarn. Be conscious, though, of when they're too busy. Keep up to date with what's going on around the land. Get to know the family. If you plan any unusual hunting (lamping for example) let the owner know beforehand.

I generally park where my Jeep is visible so it's known that I'm on the land. I also place a small plaque in the windscreen stating 'On land with permission' and giving my mobile phone number. If you intend to drive onto the land, clear it first with the owner. Don't assume that they will welcome your vehicle ploughing around the margins. Make sure you don't block gateways or access points with your vehicle. I made that mistake once and once only. The call I received from the farmer left my ears ringing and the mocking I

government officials) that your presence in pursuit of wild creatures with a firearm is legitimate.

Keep the note brief. I've seen some very complicated permission notes drawn up but in my experience, landowners dislike them. You want a few lines that the landowner can read and understand immediately and sign on the spot. If you give them something that looks like a double-glazing contract they will treat it like one. They will want to take it away, read it and call you back. You'll never hear from them again.

Mine states '*I (landowner) give Ian Barnett permission to hunt small vermin on my land, by night or day, and to remove the catch*'. Signed, dated... simple.

got from the farmhands when I'd trudged back to the motor, half an hour later, was humbling to say the least!

If you a run a dog with you, ensure it's under close control and rock-solid on stock. Stock worrying will get instant eviction from the land, and rightly so. Always carry a leash in case you need to tie your dog.

Never bring guests onto the land without the sanction of the owner. I'm lucky in that all my permissions allow both my dog and my son on the land too. If I want to invite anyone else (even from my own family) I will make a phone call in advance.

Report anything unusual (fly-tipping, signs of poaching, trespassers, sick animals). I have often politely evicted intruders

Don't forget your landowner at Christmas!

and redirected lost walkers. I have been challenged myself on many occasions, sometimes by new farm hands – and fair play to them. And, unbelievably, by the public, who shouldn't even be there.

One lady, letting her terriers run riot in private woodland where I was shooting squirrels, took exception to my appearance from behind a tree and to my rifle (slung over my shoulder, disarmed) and said she would call the police on her return home. I took out my permission note and mobile phone, called the farmer and asked if he had given permission for her to walk on his land (which he denied).

I then dialled up the number for the local police and offered her the phone. 'Press the green button, Madam, and we can settle this matter with the police now. Your dogs are out of control, which is illegal, and you are trespassing'. She stomped off in a fit of pique, never to be seen again.

Remember to keep an eye on the neighbour's land too. That quick phone call to alert the farmer to contact his neighbour could also win you more permission.

Some minor maintenance won't go amiss and will also benefit you: the path cleared of windfall branches; the gate hinges and catch sprayed with some WD40 to stop it squeaking; the fallen fence post, knocked over by the leaping deer, righted (and reported) to stop the sheep escaping. Informing the farmer of a sick animal, passing on intelligence about local issues (gossiping!), supporting them with events such as hosting the local fox-hunt.

There are many ways to thank your host for their permission to shoot. Remember, too, an extra pair of trusted eyes and hands on a large acreage is always welcome.

Never forget that a regular bottle of spirit or wine, perhaps some chocolates for the good lady or children, as a thank-you, is normally welcome. I often pass down young Sam's toys and books as he outgrows them. I shall look forward to passing down an airgun or two as well and teaching my host's children to shoot them. It will be a pleasure to help start a new generation of shooters.

Above all, remember that permission to shoot on another persons land is a tremendous, hard-won privilege and you have been gifted with an enormous level of trust. Treat it as such.

Snowdrops and peacocks

Every now and then that goddess of hunting, Diana, blesses me with her smile. There is an estate nearby which I have long coveted for shooting permission. It's an 'old money' spread covering a thousand acres, combining farm, cattle meadows, crops, hall, gardens, river and five or six woods. Owned by a peer of the realm, I hadn't got near this place despite several politely written pleas.

Then, suddenly, it came my way as the return of a favour.

One of the farms I shoot had been having trouble with a herd of fallow deer, forty strong, which had plundered the maize during last summer. When a reputable deer-stalker offered his services the farmer, Oliver, surprisingly phoned me to ask if it was alright for this chap to shoot his land. I was astounded. 'It's your land, Oliver!' I reminded him. 'Yeah, but I've given you the shooting permission, Ian.'

Shared shooting land

We both agreed that the herd needed controlling and I don't do powder-rifles, so it was a logical move, so long as we didn't end up shooting each other! Oliver said he'd get the chap to call me. David, the stalker who was obviously eager, called ten minutes later. After a long chat, during which David explained that he didn't want to encroach on another shooter's land if it would upset them, we agreed to let each other know when we would be on the land. I had no objection because we both shoot different disciplines.

David wouldn't touch the small vermin, but he has the tools to deal with deer and fox so they were his for the taking. Over the next few weeks, we exchanged texts and calls in the interest of safety. During these calls, David told me that he had the deer rights on the Hall (the estate mentioned earlier) and they were having trouble with squirrels: would I be interested? You bet!

A pattern started to emerge. I tend to shoot Oliver's land afternoons and evenings (squirrels, corvids, pigeons, rabbits). David was focussing on dawn stalking to thin the fallow. I called him and said 'Let's make this easy: you take the mornings, I'll take the afternoons and if we have a need to change the pattern, then we call each other'. It's working fine. Then, one Saturday, David called me to say that the Lady at the Hall wanted to meet me about the squirrels. 'When?' I asked. 'How about tomorrow... I'm over there?'

Pre-shoot nerves

Now I'm usually a very confident guy. I should be. I run an £8 million budget in the day job. I manage around 200 people, regularly give presentations, address public forums and I have held hundreds of job interviews when recruiting staff. I've been interviewed myself many, many times and I know how to handle myself in front of a board of directors. So why did I feel so damn nervous that Saturday night? My wife thought it was hilarious. 'What should I wear?' 'How do I address her?' 'Should I take the gun?' I called David for advice. He laughed too. 'Don't bring the gun, dress country casual, bring your insurance documents and don't worry, the Lady is very down to earth!' Despite this, I didn't sleep much. This was, in many ways, more important than a job interview. This was a one-off chance to gain shooting permission on a shooter and photographer's Nirvana, close to home and, just as importantly, to help make a difference on this estate. In terms of my 'secondary' career as a freelance writer and photographer, I was

sure that this little piece of Britain would have everything I needed (and more) regarding flora and fauna.

Next morning, I cleaned and 'dubbined' my shooting boots. That was a first! Overnight, I'd even considered wearing my business suit but convinced myself that the Lady wouldn't take me seriously as a pest controller, and David would have died laughing! So, when I met David at the entrance to the Hall, I was in country greens. As he'd already been stalking, he was head to foot in camouflage. I felt underdressed. Despite all the calls, this was the first time David and I had met face-to-face. I told David that I felt like the 'keeper's boy' going for his first job interview. We were of a similar age (the wrong side of 50) so I was amused when he said 'Don't worry, boy, you'll do fine'! I liked this guy. In we went, and driving down to the Hall I was looking around me like a child in a sweet shop. With the leaf off the trees, I could see old magpie and crows nests, and dreys aplenty. Woodpigeon fluttered atop the ivy-strangled beeches as our two vehicles crawled down the drive, respecting its 10 mph speed limit.

David walked me around to the kitchen entrance and the Lady opened the door to us. Our offer to kick off the boots was waved away and we were invited in. What I didn't get was an 'interview'. I was introduced and then the Lady and David talked about local issues while I stood (with my cap between folded hands) and contributed to the conversation where I could. I knew

Squirrel cull at the Old Hall

some of the folk they were discussing. I have permission with some, have been refused by others, so I was 'on-guard' a little. One particular line of talk intrigued me, about a couple of local environmental issues. I would never dare to put an age on the Lady, for fear she would read this and never forgive me. But this conversation alone told me that here stood a pocket-dynamo, instrumental and influential in many local decisions. I had immediately warmed to her, but would she accept me? David explained that I had insurance documents with me and she looked at them briefly. The Lady simply asked 'So, you like to shoot squirrels, do you?'

To which I replied 'Yes', and immediately regretted my answer for I wouldn't shoot any creature unless it was necessary, because its presence was a nuisance or compromising the existence of another creature. Which is what I wished I'd said. Luckily, the moment passed without comment. We chatted about access times and the Lady asked me to confine my visits to between dawn and dusk, and to call before coming. Within weeks, as the trust built, this last protocol was waived.

Tour of the Estate

David then gave me the grand tour. We talked as we walked around the woods and fields, me struggling to keep up with the stalker's long strides. I spotted a pair of roe deer watching us, statuesque, from a covert and David complimented me on my hunter's eye. The tour was delightful, more-so in the company of another 'man-of-the-woods'. What a diverse estate. I was looking forward to starting work.

On my first solo visit I didn't shoot at anything, I just explored the whole estate again, noting where dreys and corvid nests were while the leaf was down. I marked the pigeon flight-lines. I found where the pheasants were taking cover and where the peacocks were concentrated, both to be protected from airgun fire.

Over the next few weeks I concentrated my shooting around the Garden Wood: an ornamental copse below the big house planted with beech, ash, cherry, larch, spruce, oak, laburnum and rhododendron. This area was to be the focus of the Hall's 'Snowdrop Walks' soon and they were budding. I had immediately spotted the link between squirrel activity and the burgeoning carpet of white flowers. The sweet, succulent bulbs had provided sustenance for the greys during the hardest winter in ten years. The digging and delving was evident.

On my first shooting visit I took out six grey squirrels in two hours, four without leaving the cover of a single tree-trunk.

Next time, four more: from the same small area. By now Ralph, the gardener, had asked me for tails for a fly-fishing friend who tied his own flies. No problem. On the third visit, only two tails – but four squirrels and a worry. My FAC-rated HW100K has huge stopping power. Silent but deadly. Two squirrels had expired where they sat, across ivy-covered boughs above the snowdrops. Even extra shots wouldn't dislodge them. All next day, the final 'Snowdrop Walk' day, I had visions of one of those stiff corpses falling at the feet of a visitor.

Later that evening, the sound of peacock calls resounded in my head. I could swear the birds were crying *'Uppp theeerre! Uppp theeerre!'*

A guardian of the Old Hall

Whisperwood Casserole

A real winter-warmer, this one. Four tiny pellets buy all the meat you'll need. Shoot two rabbits and two woodpigeons. With the rabbits, cut the best meat off the saddle and hind legs. Use only the rich pigeon breasts. I always casserole wild meat in a slow cooker for a real 'melt in the mouth' result. On a crisp January Sunday, this can all be thrown in the pot before you leave the house at dawn to go hunting. When you return, cold and hungry, you'll open the door to the rich aroma of this delicious concoction.

Ingredients (Serves four)

2 rabbits (saddles & hindquarters)
Breasts of 2 pigeons
1 large onion
Button mushrooms
Mixed peppers
1 tin of chopped tomatoes
1 packet of Sausage Casserole mix
A sprinkling of salt and pepper
A dash of Worcester sauce

Whisperwood caserole

1 large spoonful of onion gravy granules

1 glass red wine (optional)

250 ml of water

Plain flour

Preparation

Slice the onion, mushrooms and cleaned-out peppers straight into the cook-pot. Now add everything else except the meat and flour.

Bone the rabbit portions and just use the best, tender parts of the saddle and hind-quarters. Wash and cube the rabbit meat and pigeon breasts then dust lightly in the flour. Stir fry in hot oil for 5 minutes to seal the texture, then add to the cook-pot. Give it all a good stir. The red wine is optional but I use it on the basis that once you've opened the bottle, it's a shame to waste the rest! It'll be quite inviting by the time you serve up.

Cooking and serving

Set the slow cooker on a low setting then go out to shoot some more rabbits and pigeons if you can. The beauty of the slow cooker is that you don't have to worry what time you get back. It won't burn or over-boil. When you return, turn the setting to high for 2 hours. Peel some potatoes for mashing and prepare some Yorkshire puds or dumplings.

While the potatoes are boiling you may want to add a couple of spoonfuls of the flour to thicken the sauce, as slow-cooking can tend to be a bit watery.

Serve with creamy mashed potatoes, garden peas and the Yorkshire puds or dumplings.

Oh... and don't forget the rest of that bottle of red wine!

A perfect recipe for the slow-cooker

March

Yearning

The march of winter now comes to its peak
And bird and beast and Hunter, solace seek
From soggy boot, wet fur and frozen feather
From harsh hunger and from wet and squally
weather.
The merest hint of change would raise the heart
The sign of nesting bird, the blossoms start
The Hunter sits and hones the blunted knife
Waiting for the flush of Spring's new life.

Dog and gun

This is a time of wind and wet squalls, when hunting days are a challenge with an air rifle. Not that it stops me going out. I've never been precious about my guns: if they get wet I just strip them and dry them. A wipe of gun oil, a smear of grease and a bit of TLC keeps them in order. They're a tool, nothing more.

There is, though, another tool in my 'basket of interventions' against vermin which requires a far higher level of maintenance. So when the weather slows down the shooting I always take the opportunity to carry out the annual service. No, I'm not talking about the Jeep. I'm talking about my lurcher, Dylan.

When, after some years in that wilderness called 'career progression', my wife and I decided that there was time in life for a dog, I had only one type in mind. Back out in the fields again, with my hunting head on, I seriously missed having a hound by my side. As a kid, I was denied dogs: my parents weren't interested. In fact, my father had a fear of them. In my teens, with income and independence, I coveted one.

When I had my own house, I could have one (or two, or three) and they were always going to be a hunting breed. Not for me, though, the yapping terrier or the wayward spaniel. Not the lovable Labrador or the (then) fashionable Staffie. I knew exactly what dog I would get. It is said that dogs resemble their owners (so perhaps I'm flattering myself a bit here) but I was captivated by the history and the dark romanticism of the gypsy cur, the poacher's stealthy companion: the lurcher.

Inseparable – man and dog

45

I spent hours of my spare time running a trio of ridiculously diverse lurcher breeds (not a story for here) at rabbit and hare. The training was haphazard, amateur. I was young and immature. So were the dogs. But it sowed a seed.

Five years ago when I had a tiny lurcher pup in the house again, I was determined that he would be schooled to the full – patiently and positively – until I had the hunting companion I wanted at my side in the field. As I was full into air rifle hunting, this was a big ask and attracted criticism from various quarters. The lurcher, with its gazehound ancestory, is a chasing dog, some said. Air rifle work is about stealth and patience. I chose to ignore the apparent dichotomy, for good reason. If all the recollections are true, the real lurcher was 'conceived' as a notion by poachers of old who needed a cross-breed which would be fast, agile and obedient.

My kind of dog

That old ne'er-do-well ambling down a country lane on his way home from the alehouse, dog at his side, needed a cur that would leap the farmers gate, steal into the hen house and meet him further up the lane with supper in its mouth. That was the sort of dog that appealed to me (not the stealing bit, I might add!). A dog that could be trained into thinking ahead and understanding what would please his Master.

A dog that can be restrained from chasing even its legitimate quarry, with a mere whisper or flick of the finger, yet could launch itself like a missile when asked to. A silent dog that barks only at a direct threat. A dog that can jump a fence or gate. A dog that will retrieve quarry when asked to. A dog that will dispatch quarry when instructed to. That was why I chose my lurcher: a Bedlington/whippet and deerhound/greyhound cross. Sight, speed, coat and intelligence, the latter coming from his Bedlington grandfather.

Dog training basics

Selecting a pup is always a lottery. I was lucky, but it took me three years to realise it. Dylan trained well into the basics. Sit, lay, come back, stay – though I had some serious setbacks. Early retrieving was random and he still won't retrieve feather. Heel training was difficult: it always is

Dylan, my Deerhound/Greyhound x Bedlington/Whippet

with a dog that walks much faster than you can. So we learned to compromise and Dylan ranges a few feet in front but comes immediately behind the gun at the flick of a finger or a hushed *'Get here!'*

The *'Stay!'* command came with time and by increasing distance and duration gradually, patiently. Similarly, jumping was introduced slowly and still rarely used. It's useful to teach a pup to cross a barrier but more useful to allow it to find an alternative, a detour. How many lurcher owners have lost their dog due to insisting on a kamikaze approach to hurdling, blind to hazards on the other side?

Flushing out hand signals were down to his intelligence, not my training skills. He soon reasoned that a wave and *'Look about!'* in one direction or other meant that's where I knew the quarry to be. He learned by default, and watched many an escaping rabbit or rat before the penny finally dropped.

One of the most difficult, yet crucial, instructions was the *'Leave!'* command. Gaining permission to shoot over farmland is precious and can be so easily lost if you have a dog that worries stock or chases poultry. Though it took time, I now have a hound who can be restrained from all the temptations in front him. It is doubly important when shooting, for to run in front of my rifle could cost him his life. So he was taught to *'Leave'* almost every type of creature at my signal, even his natural quarry.

This was to prove a huge bonus when,

sadly, the Hunting Act was passed. I said 'almost' everything? I can still never, ever trust my lurcher to ignore a cat. The inbred pathological hatred is serious, almost comical and cartoon-like, but many farms have cats so it is a problem.

Today was a training 'check' day. It involved running the dog through his paces and reminding him that the right to accompany me in the field isn't a 'given'. He needs to pass a few tests and some of these

Dylan, who I managed to train into a good shooting companion

disciplines are easily forgotten, or worse still, ignored, if not applied regularly.

Opening the tailgate of the Jeep is normally his cue to jump out and nose about so today, as I open it, I tell him to 'Stay'. He looks puzzled but obeys and lies, watching, in the back as I ready my gear.

A flick of the fingers and he drops down to heel next to me. We set off. Walking up the edge of the wood I release him with a 'Go on!', his cue to free-range. While he's distracted, nosing about, I sneak the fur-wrapped dummy from the game bag and drop it into a bush.

We walk on a bit and I call him to me and let him sniff my hands. His ears come up and his tail wags. 'Go fetch!' and off he goes, back down the trail, scenting the air. He pounces into the hedgerow and trots back with the dummy in his jaws, ragging it as he comes. I reward him with a small meat-treat and give him a pat.

At the top corner of the copse, I tell him to 'Drop' (his lie-down command) and 'Stay'. It is far more comfort-

A good retrieve this time; but it isn't always so!

to pass me at speed I say 'Steady!' and he slams on the brakes. 'Get here!' brings him back to heel and we walk on, playing the dummy game a few more times. Into the wood and I approach a fallen stump. 'Over!' – he hurdles it and I clamber over too.

Down the hill to a meadow and I tell him to jump the rabbit netting. Stalking up the field's edge, a cock pheasant sprints

able for a boney running dog to lie than to sit. I walk around the corner, out of sight and amble along the wood's edge about a hundred yards., then whistle lightly. He comes thundering around the corner, skidding, and sprints to me. As he makes

out of the hedgerow. The dog bristles, paw in the air, ears forward. 'Leave!' – he relaxes. 'Drop!' – he lies down.

We sit quietly at the fence. After a time, Dylan's ears stand up and his dark, damp nostrils quiver excitedly. A coney emerges to graze a few feet from the fence. The dog half-rises. *'Drop'*, I whisper lightly and he does. About 35 yards and a sitter to a kneeling shot. As I'm about to tickle the trigger, I whisper *'Leave!'* If I don't, he will be chasing the pellet to its target.

The rabbit flips and does that strange little stutter as all the senses shut down, the dog watching intently. *'Go fetch!'* and in he races to retrieve the rabbit. He trots back and holds the rabbit in his mouth about six feet from me, reluctant to give it up. I pull a reward from my pocket. *'Dead!'* I remind him, holding out the treat. The dog walks in to swap the quarry for the treat. Well, it worked this time (but doesn't always!)

On the return to the Jeep, I edge him through the horse paddock, past the farmer's mares. Dylan jogs nervously at my side, almost hiding behind me. The older mare starts to bob toward us, threatened

A well-earned rest after hunting

by the dog's presence, so Dylan bristles and starts toward the horse. *'Leave!'* – harshly this time – and he comes around behind me again but his eyes never leave the huge horse.

Crawling under the gate a friendlier face appears. It's Bundy, the farm dog. I release Dylan with a *'Go on!'* and he goes to greet the cattle dog. They sniff each other and run about for a while, the livestock now ignored.

As I watch him enjoying the older bitches company, I reflect sadly that in just a few more years I've got to find another pup to train up behind him. I just pray that I'm as astute in my choice next time, for the newcomer will have huge boots to fill. He's a good lad: all tests passed today.

The tools and the result

Sorry, Dad!

If pups learn best from old dogs and if the same theory is applied to humans, why then is succession management so difficult?

Shooting with a youngster

Young Sam shows only a passing interest in the countryside and even less in the arts of shooting and hunting. Perhaps it's that old adage: too much of a good thing? My son had access to shooting, legally supervised at all times, from a very early age.

Where I, as a youngster, had to move heaven and earth to satisfy the hunting gene (often illicitly, I confess), Sam has opportunity aplenty and turns it down with disdain. Though he ventures out with me on occasion (and today is one of

Sam has the capability, but not always the will!

those rare trips) I never try to force him out. It has to be voluntary or not at all.

Those who know me will testify that I'm definitely not a patient man where most things are concerned. I rush through life with a passion to achieve and succeed, a trait which has served me well in my career but must frustrate many folk caught up in the tail-wind. My restlessness spills over into my private life and I'm rarely still. A few hours in a cinema finds me itching to move around, a couple of hours reading a book is an hour too much and as for relaxing in front of the TV? Forget it. I love sport but even a big football match is watched in snatched moments as I move from project to project.

The only time I show any inclination towards tranquility is when I'm perched behind a net with a camera and a gun. Then I will sit for hours and just watch the natural world go by. Sam has a similarly short concentration span but could break world records in immobility... happily lolling in an armchair, lost in a two dimensional world of PC gaming, text messaging, television and that surreal universe we call communication, the Internet.

Today, much to my surprise, he had agreed to come shooting. So I took a deep breath, knowing that this would be yet another test of my patience, and told him to look out his hunting wear and find his boots. I glanced at the lurcher, already cart-wheeling around the house because he'd heard the word *'shooting'*. Against all my better judgement, I told Sam to grab

Teaching Sam stance and elevation

the dog's lead too. As we left, my wife threw me a knowing smile and bid me 'Have fun!' She'd seen it all before.

Target practice

First was some target practice. I wanted Sam to get his eye in again and we had both decided it would be fun to stick with the spring guns today. I shoot these too rarely now yet I know, from experience, that a regular session with a springer will improve my own shooting technique.

We set some targets out along the edge of a copse and I checked zero on my old BSA Lightning carbine. Bang on at 30 yards and it hadn't seen the light of day in almost a year. This light little gun is an ideal weight for Sam and he soon got his eye in again, with me pacing about behind him giving a running lecture on breathing technique, follow-through and how to balance the gun.

It's not easy for the lad. I'm a dreadful teacher. Lord help him when it comes to driving lessons! Soon he is rocking the metal crow spinner at 30 yards like an old pro. My Weihrauch HW97K is a much heavier under-lever rifle. No zero problem here either and it is punching both the crow target and a 40 yard metal rabbit-head easily.

Sam was enjoying the plinking (so was I) and he was also remembering his safety lessons, holding the broken barrel while he loaded a pellet, cocking the gun away from both the dog and me and checking that the lurcher was behind him before he shot. Next I had him try some variations: standing shots, prone shots and elevations.

He tried out the HW97K but found it too much for him so he went back to the Lightning. Satisfied that he was shooting well and safely, it was time to go hunting.

As we were going to work as a 'hunting pack', I figured that some grey squirrel culling was the best option. So we headed for a reliable copse. I parked about half a mile away. The lurcher jumped out of the Jeep excitedly when he realised we were ready for action. Sam was still in the motor.

'Aren't we driving there, Dad?' he asked.

'It's only half a bloody mile, boy! We're going to walk up there quietly'.

Half way there, I was looking over my shoulder at a teenager dragging the weight of his size 8 boots through the grass with all the enthusiasm of a red-carded footballer heading for the tunnel. The look on his face was the same too.

Team shooting precautions

At the wood's edge I passed him the Lightning, cocked and loaded, safety on. I told him not to touch the safety catch unless told to by me.

I'm right-handed, so I asked Sam to follow at my right shoulder, rifle muzzle down. I told him to walk when I walk, stop when I stop. We entered the gloomy copse, still devoid of leaf cover and started a five-step stalk towards its centre. I trod quietly across the damp leaf-mulch, avoiding the twigs I could see and paused on every fifth step to scan the wood ahead.

The dog was ranging a few steps in front. Every time I stopped, I heard Sam continue behind. It wasn't hard to tell he was still moving because for every five steps he took, he broke three twigs underfoot. The scowls thrown over my shoulder were wasted, as he wasn't watching me. I stopped and gave him a quick talk about how acute our quarry's hearing was and how silence was crucial to hunting.

'Sorry, Dad!'

We moved on, but not far. Sam had decided that the best way to avoid treading on dead wood was to kick all the leaf mulch away before he walked over it. If looks could kill, I'd just murdered him!

I glimpsed a flash of fluffy tail on the ground about fifty yards off so I raised my hand to halt Sam and glanced behind me. He'd disappeared! 'Sam!' I whispered loudly 'Where are you?'

A bright face popped around a tree trunk, grinning. 'Sorry, Dad. Needed a wee!' He re-appeared, empty handed. 'Sam, where's your gun?' I hissed. 'Whoops... Sorry, Dad!' Back he went. The squirrel had long gone.

Further on and we were doing alright. Quiet, stealthy progress. Suddenly the lurcher looked behind me, his ears pricked up and he reared up like a startled pony. Then he went sprinting off to my left, to catch the branch that Sam had just thrown for him. He snatched it up and went haring off in those huge sweeping circles that a released lurcher enjoys, before bringing it back to Sam. The dog was panting hard, his tail wagging. Meanwhile, wood pigeon had clattered from boughs, a rabbit had bolted for cover and the treetops were alive with scrabbling as squirrels leapt away in all directions. Sam was holding his rifle by the scope and the barrel was pointing at the sitting dog.

They say one of the golden rules when training a pup is never to chastise it when you're trying to train it and it doesn't quite get the task right. No-one ever said that rule applied to young boys with guns. I went ballistic. The poor lad got the rollicking of his life and I should think every squirrel for two counties could hear me. His excuse? 'Sorry, Dad. Dylan looked bored!'

Father and son

Have you ever seen a lurcher look bored while hunting squirrels? The 'hunting' session was over.

On the trek back to the motor I was still lecturing that 'many lads would give their right arm to be out with a gun blah, blah, blah.' Sam paced beside me with disappointing vigour in his step. I was wasting my breath. 'What's for dinner, Dad?' he asked.

'Not bloody squirrel, that's for sure!' I spat back. Then we grinned at each other and I put an arm around his shoulder as we walked back. It's only hunting and obviously not for him, I reasoned inwardly. He's a good lad at heart.

'Let's pick up a Chinese on the way back,' I said and he raced the dog back to the Jeep.

When the wild wind blows

At this time of year the almost constant wind makes for a difficult time with the air rifle. Relying on its relatively light ammunition, accuracy becomes a black art, choosing the moment to shoot between gusts and learning how to compensate for any breeze. I'd rather face this challenge, though, than shelve the gun simply because conditions are less than perfect. After all, my farmers would still expect some pest control to be carried out and the lurcher, like me, doesn't handle the psychology of confinement well. We both climb the walls. Sure, we can go out and about, but to me a walk around the countryside without a gun is like that interminable waste of time they call 'golf', a good walk spoiled. So I've been shooting the breeze, with a little help from some excellent kit and not a little previous experience.

We've just emerged from the hardest winter in over ten years out in the East, and the signs are that there will be a significantly reduced rabbit population this year. Nature has a way of restoring balance, does it not? Previous mild winters have encouraged rabbits to breed all year round and I have seen kits in every month of the year. I haven't seen any during this harsh January and February though. It's as though the adults could sense the imminent harsh weather and their hormones shut down for a while. This won't surprise many hunters, for wild things often tell us what the Met Office dare not commit to.

Back in January, I was taking my son from Norwich to Cambridge in the Jeep one day. It was around mid-day. The forecast was for 'wintery showers' that night. On the trip down the A11 it was obvious to me that they'd got it wrong. I pointed out to Sam the hundreds of coneys out feeding, despite the grey sky and icy wind, along the verges and in the cattle meadows. Further along, on the Elveden estate, we saw roe deer feeding on winter crops, blatantly ignoring the danger of such exposure. At Elveden crossroads, we were amazed to see a muntjac browsing beneath the traffic-lights. I warned Sam we were in for very hard weather. Sure enough, that night we had the heaviest snowfall for three years. A week later, East Anglia (and much of the country) was hit by its worst snow in 20 years.

Advantages of snow

Now, I have to say this was all useful. Thanks to the snow I now had more intelligence about my shoots and their hidden occupants. Those tracks and trails have exposed hidden warrens, showed me where the fox walks and the stoat hunts. The pigeon roosts shifted to escape the keen easterlies. Squirrel highways were exposed and I even know where the magpie takes a drink, its tracks to the pool captured in the frozen, white coating. Useful knowledge, to be put to good use when this damn wind abates!

Effects of wind on shooting

I am, of course, being a bit defeatist in cursing the wind as a blight to the hunter. There are times when it can assist the shooter. It is a poor combatant who can't use the strengths of the enemy to their own advantage. Using the breeze to stalk carefully to within shooting range of a browsing animal is familiar to most shooters.

As we learn the wind (and its fickleness) we learn how to read other effects too. Its impact on the land and contours as we hunt. The Westerly that has become a Northerly because of the high bank we are approaching, indicated by the bending rye grass. The flight of a crow or woodies into the spinney you are approaching conflicts with your expectation of the wind direction. You stop and check the zephyr again. There are many ways to do this. Pluck a handful of meadow grass or a few dry leaves and cast them up. Some shooters use a small 'puffer' filled with fine powder (don't use talc!). On a bitter day, your own breath will be visible. Yes, the air is in your face, but there is a wide break in the hedgerow further on. It's diverting the wind, which you can't see or smell – but your quarry certainly can.

Gusty winds, while an inconvenience to an air rifle hunter, are manageable with experience. The wind is like the sea. It has patterns and trends (and unpredictable swings in behaviour). There was an old movie where Steve McQueen played a prisoner, Papillon, on the infamous Devil's Island penal colony. It was reputedly based on a true story. Determined to escape, Papillon spent half a lifetime watching the unforgiving waves that beat at the islands cliffs. He determined that there was indeed a pattern. There would be a lull when he could throw his home-made raft into the sea and it wouldn't be smashed against the rocks. Then he could then throw himself over the cliff and swim to his raft. Papillon escaped. Shooting in blustery winds is often like this. One, two, three gusts, then a moment of calm. Two to ten seconds at most. It's simply about how to recognise and use those moments. Did I really say 'simply'?

Target shooters are masters of this art. They know how to judge 'windage' and compensate for the breeze by off-setting the shot. Rarely would these experts shoot in conditions much above a 20 mph blow. With competition target shooting, it matters little if the pellet is pulled off line. It's not a matter of injury over dispatch. For the hunter, however, it can mean the difference between killing and maiming, the latter being unacceptable.

For the hunter, too, there is the conundrum which creates a double risk. The corvid or pigeon on a bough may itself be moving. So even adjusting for the breeze can be too much of a gamble. Add to that the third factor: compensating for elevation (therefore gravity). As I said earlier, these are black arts.

So today, as I often do in windy conditions, I went out and about with the gun

The rabbit's ears and nose give it huge advantage

but confined my hunting to a creature which can use weight and gravity to resist a strong breeze. Yet it uses that breeze with its nose and ears to give it a huge advantage over the hunter. I'm referring, of course, to the rabbit.

There is a cattle pasture I regularly shoot which is a valley, therefore a wind tunnel, but shielded on its northern edge by a huge briar-covered bank, home to a huge warren. The bank is some 400 yards long and 25 yards high, with sparse cover for the stalker, except for a smattering of young oaks along its length. Such a warren would be, I suspect, a ferreter's nightmare. You could lose a ferret forever in this tangle. Today, while stalking the warren, I counted over 100 holes along the fence-line alone. Goodness knows how many lie beneath the cover of briars and bracken. I stepped into the meadow at its far corner, the strong Westerly wind in my face at first making me think that shooting would be impossible. As I followed the dog-legged fence, my concerns evaporated. As always in this valley, the wind (like water and electricity) finds the path of least resistance. As I crept forward, I watched the rooks feeding down in the valley bed. They had spotted me, scattered and battled the currents to gain height. But beneath the high bank, I could hardly discern a whisper of air current. I moved on, turned another corner and a gust hit me again. A pile of old, dry oak leaves spiralled up and away from me in a mini maelstrom. Which told me that my scent was going away from me.

I always take a pot-filler from this warren, never failed yet, but today I had my doubts despite the specialised weaponry I had with me. I settled by the fence at the next 'kink' in the borderline. Two adult coneys sat just five yards out into the meadow. Range? About thirty-five yards. I watched, amused, as their ears went up and down like those old railway signals. Every now and then a few dry leaves would spiral up and dance in the wind. The good news for me was that they landed in my direction.

I was still on the right side of both enemies: wind and rabbit. For a while, I pretended I was Papillon. As the wind gusted, the rabbit ears danced, then they settled to feed until they sensed the next series of gusts. A clear pattern, a species behaviour, and (for me) an early warning system. Thanks guys.

I had with me a lethal combination to deal with this situation: an FAC rated (24 ft/lb) Weihrauch 100K using a specialist pellet, designed to cut through the wind – the Daystate Rangemaster. So, gun at the ready, the first rabbit head goes down to feed. I have it in the scope, side on, twixt eye and ear. First quarry to the bag. Moving down the fence the success continued. All this on a day when many air gunners may have said, 'No way! It's too windy for air rifle shooting.'

If last year was indicative of climate change, with Sirocco-like winds (even on the warmest days) shooters of any discipline are going to have to learn how to cope with them. The wind can be either friend or foe. That's true for most weather conditions. I live to hunt.

In extreme weather, I use a simple litmus test. What would the fox, probably Britain's most instinctive hunter, do today? In a force eight gale and driving rain, if I thought Old Charlie would be curled up in his den and you can bet your life that I would be too. However, as I suspect that

A result – despite the wind

those small, hirsute pads will be trotting towards my shooting permissions and my warrens, I'll be out there too. If he can hunt, so can I.

I leave you with a simple question. Before the advent of the gun, did the bowman fear the wind? Did the archer go hungry because the breeze was strong? I rest my case.

Coney Curry

They say that the Indian curry, in all its manifestations, is now Britain's most popular meal. How many people have tried it with Britain's most abundant, natural meat? Many of my colleagues think nothing of visiting a restaurant or take-away for a meal, with no idea of what's gone into the dish they're being served.

If Old Charlie can hunt in the wind – so can you

They just like the outcome and don't ask too many questions. Put a rabbit stew in front of them and just watch their noses turn up. So this is a simple, spicy 'hunters' concoction which will disguise the meat and is best simmered in a slow cooker to allow the sauce to seep fully into the meat. Ideally, prepare it and start slow cooking at mid-day for a delicious evening meal.

Ingredients (Serves 6 to 8)

2 mature rabbits
    (saddles & hindquarters)
Punnet of mushrooms
4 large potatoes
Mixed peppers
One jar of Karai (curry) sauce
Supermarket Indian snackpacks
    (onion bhaji's & samosas)
Plain naan bread
1lb easycook basmati rice
Salt & pepper
250 ml of water
2 tablespoons of cooking oil
Plain flour

Preparation

Slice the mushrooms, peel and finely cube the potatoes, wash and slice the peppers, then place them all straight into the cook-pot. Add the water and the Karai sauce.

Bone the rabbit portions, using only the lean meat from the saddle and hind

Coney Curry in prospect

legs. Wash and dice the rabbit meat, then pat it dry in a kitchen towel. Dust the meat lightly in the plain flour. Then stir-fry in the hot cooking oil for 5 minutes to seal the texture. Drain the oil and place in the cook-pot. Add some salt & pepper. Give it all a good stir.

Cooking and Serving

Slow cook on a low setting with the lid on for a minimum 4 hours. The advantage of a slow cooker is that you can go off and get on with other things. Go shooting or fishing, go to a football match, go shopping (that will impress the wife), go down the pub, whatever. Just bring your friends back and don't tell them what you're about to serve up. Simply tell them they've got curry.

When you do get back, take the lid off the pot and turn onto high for an hour to boil off and thicken up.

Heat up the oven 30 minutes before you're ready to serve up and start boiling a large pan of water for the rice (you need half a cup of rice and one full cup of water for each hungry mouth). If the Karai still looks a bit watery, add a couple of spoonfuls of flour and stir thoroughly. This will thicken the sauce. Simmer the rice and warm the bhaji's/samosa's for about 12/15 minutes before serving. Make sure you don't forget to sprinkle a little water over the naans and warm them last (for 3 minutes).

Serve up with chilled white wine or ice cold lager and watch your friends snaffle it down. Later, when you're all enjoying the after-glow of good food and good company, you might be tempted to let them know they've just eaten the finest organic, unprocessed, free-range meat that the British countryside can produce. But if you want help with the washing-up, I would advise you to keep your secret.

Coney Curry is served

April

Control

The beak that bends the twig to build the nest
Will also seek to feed its offspring best
And chaffinch chicks in bed of woven moss
Ignore the magpies talon at their loss.
The Hunter sits afar to watch the scene
Looking where he can, to intervene
The silenced guns report gives short release
And songbird parents tend their young in peace.

Mercy and murder

If all of the corvid family are notoriously difficult to control, it is because of their keen eye and natural suspicion. Placing a single terminal pellet in the relatively small kill-zone of any species of corvid is for proficient shooters only. Getting close enough to achieve this, or getting them close to you, requires experience and field-craft.

There is one time of year, though, when they are at their most vulnerable: nest building time. With the pressure of

The rookery is a busy place in April

constructing a home for their brood and the pre-occupation of gathering material, their survival instincts reach a low while paternal instincts hit a high. Both can be combined to good effect for the hunter.

Branch shooting

The rookery is busy again but I will leave it alone, perhaps to visit in May after young branchers. Perhaps not, as it is hardly 'sport' to cull young rooks stretching their wings for the first time. If only magpies did the same thing! This country tradition is a way to thin the numbers, I grant, and many a youngster has learned the art of shooting elevations in this way. Long may it continue. I have no axe to grind with this long-established rural tradition; it's just not for me. Perhaps hypocritically, I will not hesitate to cull adult rooks at the crop when given the chance, though that opportunity is rare because they are too wary. Today, watching them rebuilding and patching old nests, I am fascinated by their labour and their community spirit. They are the alter-ego of their cousins, the carrion crow and the magpie.

Magpie nest-building

I would have no compunction about shooting young magpies on the branch – if only they sat out, like rooks, stretching and exercising their wings. But they don't.

Watching the magpies building a home, I have the rifle to hand and loaded. I'm in deep cover and concealed, head to toe, in full leaf camouflage. The snood pulled up over my cheeks and nose ensures only my eyes peep from beneath the peak of my hood.

The construction is just as frantic as was the rooks. The energy required by the magpie, however, is double that of its cousins for two reasons. Firstly, many magpie pairings play the same silly game as the tiny wrens. They will start to construct two, three, sometimes four nests. Most will be half-hearted affairs and they will select one to complete and in which to breed.

In winter the magpie is a gregarious bird, flocking in numbers. During spring mating time, though, the pair will be isolated and fiercely territorial. In summer and autumn they will be flocking again but these tend to be family groupings. Watching this pair today, I stay the gun to appreciate their industry, though shoot them I will, given time. I mentioned two

Magpies need controlling before the songbirds fledge

In full camo on magpie watch

The wood in which I hide, a mere eight acres, used to be devoid of songbirds due to predation by squirrels and magpies. I will not tolerate either, now that birdsong has returned. Impressed by the display I have been watching, my loyalty is with the conservation of all those small birds who will soon start their own nests, watched

A half-finished magpie nest

reasons why their building requires great energy. The second is due to the design of their nest. Unlike the open platform of the rook, crow or jay, the magpie builds a domed fortress which requires a different level of engineering. Like the rook, they hop around the woodland floor snatching up dead twigs for the base. The roof, however, needs pliable and often living material to weave into place.

Watching a magpie twisting and scything willow or ash shoots using just claw and beak, in the way we would snap a coarse wire, illustrates why the blackbird or songthrush fledgling doesn't stand a chance of withstanding its attack.

With the roof in place the pair set about gathering dead leaves, sheep fleece from the meadow and horse hairs from the barbed wire to line the interior.

by this avaricious pair. As one of the pair drops to the floor to grab another twig, I deprive it of its partner, which goes wild.

One magpie down
It flights down to the base of the nesting tree, chattering loudly, then (in a common magpie trait) corkscrews around the trunk and back up to the nest, shrieking as it goes. The cross-hairs of my scope are already up there, waiting. As it perches on the top of the nesting tree, still complaining loudly. I shoot it and it tumbles down through the branches to land close to its mate.

I have a pang of regret. Not uncommon, having shot such a handsome bird. Then a cock blackbird, disturbed by the clamour, sounds his alarm call and flashes away to warn the rest of the copse that death is in the air. Would that he knew what I had just done for him and his mate! I pick up the two corpses and look up at the nest. A masterpiece, unfinished. As I trudge back to the Jeep I still feel guilty. But a chaffinch, trilling at the wood's edge, serenades my departure and I start to feel a little better about the assassinations. His song has been hard-won through my attentions here over the years and it's better on the ear than the guttural cackle of a thief and murderer. I study the black talons and vicious beaks at my feet. If Mother Nature deigned that both species could live here in harmony, what I had just done would have been unnecessary. But Mother Nature has a different agenda.

Hidden benefits

The need to get close to your intended quarry is essential for the air rifle hunter. Closeness ideally being within 25 to 40 yards for a proficient shooter, perhaps a bit more if you shoot an FAC-rated air rifle. You can get within those ranges through skilled stalking and fieldcraft but the price you can pay is often failure. While you are stalking, you're moving, so something (and not necessarily your quarry) may spot you. The natural defence mechanism of most birds is eyesight. The 'pipping' blackbird, the screeching jay, the fussing robin: all can alert a browsing coney, a roosting woodpigeon or a foraging squirrel.

The songbirds nest stands no chance against this tool...

...or this one

Waiting or baiting

One efficient way to get 'up close and personal' with vermin is to turn the situation around and get your quarry to come to you. This can be achieved by simply waiting long enough in the right place, or by baiting. Even so, you need be hidden away. There are five basic methods of hiding by my reckoning and, personally, I only rate four as effective. So let's take a look at each, starting with the one I don't use.

Cut your own hide

The manufactured natural hide, I say after long experience in the field, isn't worth the time and effort. We often read articles (and see in DVDs) hunters advocating the use of these. I've tried it many times. Taking a pair of secateurs, snipping off strands of natural vegetation and softwoods, building an imitation of a hedge – it all seems a reasonable way to build a hide. But think about it. You've just spent an hour or two thrashing about in the wood or hedgerow, advertising your presence to every living creature within a mile. Corvids are watching, cackling, from trees half a mile away. Woodpigeons have jinked from their flightline overhead, spooked by your presence. Rabbits are sitting nervously in the warren nearby, disturbed by your vibration. 'Don't worry,' says the man on the DVD. 'Your quarry just needs to get used to the sight of your new "hedge". Leave it for a day or two and return before dawn to hide inside.' So you do. But when you return, the fresh green construction you left two days before is now a wilted pile of dying foliage and looks like the compost heap at the bottom of your garden. Forget it. Pick up a shooting supply catalogue and read it. There are better ways to hide yourself if you can't use my first choice.

Best option: a tree

First choice: the natural hide. It's been out there in the wood or field for years, every creature is used to the sight of it and it is a living, breathing entity. Your quarry feeds, breeds, nests and shelters in it. To blend in with it you will need subtle clothing (dark, neutral clothing or perhaps camouflage) and a head-net, snood or cap won't go amiss.

Roost shooting woodpigeons is something I've done effectively for years, hidden beneath ivy-strangled trees wearing nothing but drab, dark clothing and a suntan. My own tanned, leathery visage is testament to time outdoors and I'm afraid I take about as much notice of sun-block warnings as I do the health warnings on my cigar packets. If the cigars, whisky or wine don't get me first, I'll be disappointed. I've invested a fortune in all of them. If the sun gets me, it's fair payback, as I've enjoyed its smiling face for free all of my life. There are only two endings that I fear: one is ending my life gibbering and incontinent in a home; the other is being knocked over by a LACS (League Against Cruel Sports) supporter on my way to collect the paper one morning. (If you're a LACS supporter and you're reading this, make sure you reverse over me a few times. It would be cruel to let me live.) The point being, if you've got a dark face, you won't need a net: just don't grin until you've hit your pigeon! Natural hides are prolific and can be found all year round.

All evergreens (mistletoe, holly, ivy) make excellent cover. Young conifers form an umbrella, concealing you from birds and squirrels overhead. Elder and blackthorn, too, are common and often contain niches to hide a hunter. Any fallen tree, particularly

if the roots are intact and the foliage stays verdant, is an opportunity. The obvious disadvantage with natural hides, of course, is that you can't take them to the quarry. You need your targets to come close to the hide, and that means waiting or baiting.

Second choice: fixed hide

My next best preference is the fixed-construction hide: sheep pens, pig shelters, hay barns, shepherd butts, horse stables, haystacks and silos. All, like the natural

Natural cover – my preferred option

hide, are familiar to quarry and therefore present no threat. Many quarry species flock to the farmyard, particularly in winter when food is harder to come by. On the farm, the agricultural machinery itself can be useful. Trailers allow you (if you're athletic enough) to hide underneath with an all-round view. Tractor cabs lift you up, off the ground, and out of the eyeline of ground-based vermin such as rats or rabbits.

The farmyard offers plenty of cover

Net hides

Next is the highly versatile net or leaf-blind. I use a set of four telescopic net poles with kick plate spikes that can be driven into hard ground. The poles can be adjusted to vary height according to terrain. These are carried in a slim pole bag which also has a pouch for the rolled up nets. Nowadays you can pick from a huge array of nets with patterns to suit all seasons: Advantage Timber for woodland and Max 4 for grassland, Realtree Hardwoods for the autumn copse and Hardwoods Green for the summer and spring treeline. And there are Woodland Camoreal and Moorland Camoreal leafblinds.

My growing collection of nets and blinds allows me to select the right background for most situations. Packed away: the bag, four poles and two nets weigh little more than my air rifle. They can be set up in minutes, and if you've picked the wrong spot, they can be dismantled and moved quickly. Though they don't have a roof (you can drape a net over the top), you just need to set up with a thick leaf canopy overhead and a dark background behind you. They can also be set up around a natural feature such as a tree, bush, or telegraph pole. I always carry secateurs to trim obstructions and help free snagged nets from foliage. I also carry a few tent pegs in the bag to anchor my nets in a breeze.

Flapping nets attract the attention of quarry. On many hunting trips, I don't even take the net poles. I simply pack a net into the game-bag and drape it over a fence or a gate when ambushing rabbits. But take note: you'll rarely get away with such simplicity when it comes to corvids or woodpigeons!

Pop-up hides

And so to the fifth type of hide. A development of modern technology. It is the pop-up hide. Initially an American invention, this is to the hunter what KFC is to the hungry punter: convenience concealment. I've tried several over the years and (like guns) found that you get what you pay for.

My first was a small, hooped affair in Hardwoods Green. Carried in its own circular backpack, it was fairly easy to set up but an absolute nightmare to take down. It would just never pack down in the way the instructions claimed. The roof was very low and, despite claims that it was waterproof, it leaked like a sieve. But I was sold on the concept and I took the magpies off the cow's back (as described earlier) from

Modern leaf nets can bring great results

this hide. Without it, I'd never have got near enough.

My next pop-up hide was the Ameristep Doghouse. The same basic design as the first but of much better quality. The camouflage pattern was deeper. It was rainproof, much more spacious, but I was still wrestling alligators when it came to packing away. Maybe it was just me, but it felt like cracking a Rubiks Cube. Then Deben imported the 'Hideout'. I read a review in a shooting magazine and knew I needed to have one. My wife bought me one as a birthday present, bless her.

It is the Aston Martin DBS of pop-up hides – luxurious and shaped like a wigwam. Though a bit heavier to carry than the others, it can be set up in 10 seconds, thanks to a clever internal frame system. You can take it down just as fast but fighting it into the carry bag takes a few minutes more. When erect, it has plenty of space for all my gear and I can stand up and move about in it (though, to be fair, I'm only 5' 5" tall!). The ground line pegs are solid and resist high winds. The windows are great: double-layered diamonds with an internal black-out sheet and an external camouflage gauze. These allow you see out, but nothing can see in. An excellent hide; totally waterproof too.

Pop-up hides can be moved easily to a strategic spot

Static ambush model

I've shot many rabbits, squirrels, crows and pigeons from this beauty. Like my nets, it can be moved about easily. But it is substantially heavier than my net-pole rig and I wouldn't want to trawl one about all day. This is for those planned, static ambushing sorties.

When siting a pop-up hide, I try to place it under natural cover and set the door so that I can enter and exit into cover. I only open windows as I need to; keep the vents minimal. The intention is to keep light out and your scent in. Standing and stretching regularly will keep your circulation going, crucial in the cold of winter. In summer heat, a pop-up hide can swelter inside and can attract gnats and midges, so it's a wise shooter who packs a head-net and some insect repellent. A rotating tripod seat will give you a good shooting position in such a hide (and is useful behind nets too).

Remember that setting up markers (twigs or coffee-stirrers are ideal) at your zero range will help immensely. Peeping through a hide window or leaf-blind can distort your vision and make range-finding difficult. The markers will put your judgement back into perspective.

Shooting through a net can distort your range-finding, so I use visual aids

The power game

For over thirty years I was content to employ the British legal limit (sub-12 ft/lb) rifle for vermin control work. Though I've played with shotguns and sampled small-bore rifles, I've always preferred the discretion and silence of the air rifle. The hunting game, for me, is about stalking or ambushing my quarry. Most of all, it's about being able to blend into the landscape and become one with the wildlife around me. The shotgun and small-bore rifle, effective as they are, make far too much noise for my liking.

Extended-range airgun

On many areas of land it can be impossible to get close to quarry. Some of the broad arable fields I shoot have little cover: low hedgerows, sparse coverts, spinneys and cover crops. Gradually, a desire came for some extended range, particularly to control corvids and pigeons. Pushing the range limit with sub-12 gun means compromising on accuracy. Such compromise will – on many occasions – mean injury to quarry, rather than clean dispatch. At such distances (50 yards or more) the shooter is unlikely to catch up with a 'pricked' animal or bird. So the result is a cruel death or worse still, maimed survival.

I have one 12 ft/lb air-rifle, a Weihruach HW100K, which I can reliably use out to 50 yards for clean dispatch, but conditions would have to be perfect (no breeze, no rain) and with selected pellets (no defects). I have the benefit of experience. I certainly wouldn't advocate such a distance to a beginner.

Firearms certification

Eventually, curiosity overcame me and I wanted to experiment with some extended power. Any air rifle capable of shooting above the 12 ft/lb power limit is considered a 'fire-arm' and the user needs to be licensed accordingly by their local Constabulary. Application for an FAC (Fire-Arms Certificate) is a simple process but subject to qualification. You need good reason for applying, such as vermin control. You need land suitable for the use

of such power. You need socially acceptable referees: two people willing to vouch for your good character and soundness of mind. You will be subject to a visit or two from a Firearms Licensing Officer (FLO) and must demonstrate the security of your home and that you have a compliant gun safe. They may want to check your shooting land, too.

For me, the process was swift and I can only commend Norfolk Constabulary on their administration of the application. I have to say, though, that I had been prudent enough to do some groundwork. Long before I applied, I asked the FLO around for a chat and a cup of tea. He checked the house for me and advised on security and safes. We talked over the reasons for a future application. Basically we got to know each other.

Now, there's something of a 'chicken & egg' scenario with FAC-rated guns. You can't fire one without a license. Nor can you buy one or borrow one without breaking the law. So, like many applicants before me, I 'took the ticket' and purchased my first gun.

There are relatively few FAC-rated air rifles on the market in the UK. Nor are they cheap. Ironically, you can buy a decent rimfire for around £250, capable of shooting out to 200+ yards. An FAC precharged air rifle, capable of 60/70 yards to a highly proficient shooter, will set you back between £600/£1000 – without the rifle-scope! I went for a popular 35 ft/lb model with a buddy-bottle air supply. Big mistake. Having acquired my licence, I should have tried some models first.

Not the right gun for me

Disappointed would be an understatement after spending all that money. It was noisy. I had expected extra noise at that power and had bought a high-spec moderator to reduce the sound at the muzzle. More money, so more disappointment. The accuracy even at 30/40 yards was appalling, unacceptable.

This, I suspect was due to my discomfort with the gun. The balance was all wrong. Despite hours of practice, I couldn't achieve the consistency on targets I would expect before moving on to live quarry. Just when I thought I had mastered it, I took it into a wood and shot my first squirrel with it. Then I winged the next two and went home with a feeling of guilt and inadequacy. The gun was 'parked' and I returned to my favourite HW100K. Over the next few weeks I shot dozens of rabbits and squirrels with no problem. Confidence restored, I sold the FAC rifle for half the price I'd paid for it.

Out of the blue, I got an e-mail from Dave Nicholson at Hull Cartridge, importers of the Weihrauch rifles, who was aware of my predicament. They could now offer an FAC version of the HW100K. I was straight on the phone with an order. I waited two months for delivery from Germany but when she arrived – what a sexy little gun! The FAC power meant adding about 3" to the barrel of a standard

HW100K but she still looked compact. The stock was a 'sporter', much sleeker than her little sister's thumbhole stock. The balance felt perfect. The proof of the proverbial pudding would be on the range, though, and in the field. I immediately hit a problem: ammo.

Many FAC air rifle shooters use magnum pellets: heavy 20/22 grain slugs. To me, this seems pointless as having added the power you're now dulling the knife's edge with weight. I soon found (as suspected) that the trajectories with this ammunition were similar to the lighter pellets in a sub 12 ft/lb rifle. The more hold-over (or under) you need to judge, the less accurate you will be.

I wanted a flattened trajectory so I started to experiment with lighter pellets. AA Field Diablo's proved very good at 15.2 grain, but a bit suspect beyond longer (50 yard+) distances. I tried many pellets and found that Logun Penetrators (16 grain mini-bullets) were superb and soon I was notching up kill after kill. The flat zone on my scope was one full mil-dot from 20 yards to 70 yards. Now I was in business. Or so I thought.

Next on the agenda was live quarry, and I had a real concern: over-penetration, which happened too frequently at lower ranges (15 to 20 yards). Airgun hunting relies on the dissipation of energy from pellet to vital organ to kill cleanly. A pellet passing through a creature injures but doesn't always kill immediately. If a rabbit makes it back to its burrow or a squirrel to its drey, it will almost certainly die of the wound but it will suffer first. That, to me, is unacceptable. I experienced another opposing problem too. Now and again I shot squirrels in trees and instant despatch meant they dropped dead where they were, across a branch or in a cleft. They were unrecoverable.

The more I hunted with an FAC gun, the more I realised just how often my quarry would appear within that 20 to 40 yard range which suits the sub 12 ft/lb rifle. In fact, far more often than the 60 yard corvid or rabbit.

So, though I still regularly use my FAC rifle for work on open meadows or in 'special' situations where I know I can't get close to a problem quarry through stalking, I have remained a sub 12 ft/lb hunter. I must say, too, that I've found the moderate power of the Weihrauch (24 ft/lb) gives much better accuracy than a 35–40 ft/lb gun. Perhaps because the pellet skirts are better able to cope with the blast.

Legal-limit guns give the hunter many advantages: high air economy (more shots per charge of air), close range ability, greater silence, energy dissipation on impact and (on a carbine) shorter barrels. Over a year of experimentation, my hunting journals told the story. On average, I brought back twice as much quarry in my bag on a sub-12 ft/lb hunt compared with a 24 ft/lb FAC hunt.

The FAC Weihrauch HW 100KS

From pasture to plate – and back again

Preparation of a shot rabbit will become second nature after practice. Make sure you carry a sharp knife for this purpose (I use an Opinel No.7, a £5 knife which hones to surgical precision). Always paunch your shot rabbits in the field if you intend to eat them. This makes them a hell of a lot lighter to carry about, too. Squeeze the rabbit first (to evacuate the bladder) by running your thumb down the body firmly, from rib-cage to tail. Leaving a full bladder can taint the meat and if you accidentally puncture it while paunching out (removing the entrails) you can forget it as a table offering.

Gutting in the field

Next make a shallow cut from between the back legs to the rib cage but be careful not to cut into the entrails. If you do, the contents of the colon or stomach will taint the useful meat. You will learn, through trial and error, how to judge the depth of the cut so that you open the stomach cavity without nicking the entrails.

If you've done it right, hold the coney by its front and rear legs and flip it over robustly (make sure the opening is away from you!) and eject the entrails, cutting the ends clear with your knife. If you do this violently enough, no cut will be necessary. Gravity will do the job for you. Make sure this exercise is carried out somewhere discrete and the offal left where the crows and foxes (not the farmers dog!) can find it and clean up for you.

Butchering back home

At home, lay the rabbit on a cutting board. Have a fillet knife, secateurs and colander to hand. Also, a waste bag for the unwanted parts. The skinning of a rabbit takes just a minute or two with practice. Use secateurs to clip off the back paws. Forget the front legs; unless you're desperate for meat you aren't going to use them. The prime meat of the rabbit is on its haunches and its back (saddle)

Separate the flesh around its midriff from the skin. Work your hands between flesh and fur, around the back, from either side until you have a void. Slice through the fur at this point so that you have a top and a bottom. Grab both pieces and pull in opposite directions (toward the tail and toward the head). Forget the head end. I'll tell you what to do with that later.

With one hand around the rib-cage, pull the fur of the bottom half down swiftly (imagine you're pulling off the trousers).

Now draw a sharp knife from below each lowest rib to the backbone. I also trim off the scanty skirt of flesh which looks like a wing between the rear legs and the lower rib. My lurcher loves this, flash-cooked in the microwave and added to his dinner. Cut the backbone at this point with the secateurs. This will leave the saddle and rear legs. Discard the rest.

Squeezing out

*Run the knife, blade up,
from groin to rib-cage*

The tail is still on though, so grab it firmly, twist several times and pull hard. This will draw out the tail and any remaining anal tube. This should leave you with the prime portions of meat on a rabbit: the saddle (back) and hind quarters. The rabbit is a hopping animal and relies on those powerful back legs to propel it. That's where the muscle is. The front legs, by comparison are scrawny.

Place the remainder of the rabbit on its back, break back both hind legs at the hip joint and use a sharp knife to cut from a quarter inch each side of the tail area to the hip joint. This will avoid the anal glands (cutting these will taint the meat). From the other end, cut from both sides of the thigh to the hip joint. Roll back each hip joint and it should just pop out. You now have three segments of meat: two legs and a saddle. Trim off any white, fatty membrane and on a mature rabbit you now have about half a pound of lean, organically fed meat.

I go one step further now, because I'm fussy and this is free meat. I bone out these joints. I pare all the pure, red meat from the bone, trim off any fat and cube the

Remove the back paws at the knuckle join first

Separate the fur from the flesh, right around the body

Hold the rabbit by both ends and flip it away robustly

The paunch will eject in one piece

flesh I want to retain. If I'm not cooking immediately these are stored in tubs in my freezer and used for kebabs, burgers, pies, casseroles and curries. At any one time, I probably have close to 10lb of rabbit meat at my disposal (not to mention pigeon breasts). Some is cooked for the lurcher before it slips past a reasonable storage time. Most is served to the table: 'waste not, want not'.

But what do you do with the residual waste? Well, that depends on your circumstances. The paunch you removed in the field should have been discretely tipped into a hedgerow or ditch, out of sight.

Nature has its own clean-up squad: the fox, badger, crow, magpie and stoat. I've often paunched a large amount of rabbits on a night-lamping sortie and returned to shoot at dawn to find the whole lot gone. Not a trace. You can use this to your advantage, too. If you use a regular spot to paunch, vermin will come looking, habitually, for a free breakfast. For the airgunner, this is useful. If the fox left anything for the magpie, one of the earliest risers, and you're in place before the bandit, it will pay

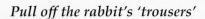

Pull off the rabbit's 'trousers'

Snip through the backbone, below the first rib. Note the skirt-flesh which can be kept for the dog

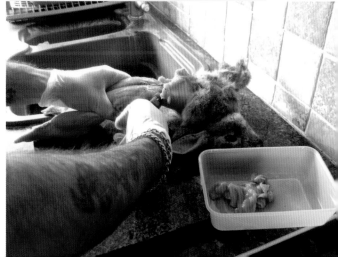

The prime meat on a rabbit, ready for boning out

the price. For this reason I usually return the detritus of a skinning session done at home to its rightful place: the wood and field. Discreetly hidden and (mutually) beneficial. Sometimes, it goes to the local raptor sanctuary or to friends with ferrets.

A freezer full of prime, organic meat

May

First Blood

All industry and clamour on the bough
As rooks fly back and forth, twixt nest and plough
And fledging clowns all jostle at the hub
Black faces crying out for seed and grub.
The young boy watches as they stretch their wings
His frail arm is raised, the airgun sings
A hue and cry breaks out above his head
As this new Hunter's first dispatch drops dead.

Egg Protection

Walking this Norfolk hinterland on a bright spring morning brings back distant memories of a care-free childhood, in a place far from here, where I learned the manner of many a bird and beast. It was an apprenticeship unrestrained by fear of harm or malice. Summers were a *Boys Own* halcyon, spent exploring the woods and fields close to the new-town where I lived. Early every morning our gang of urchins, kicked out from under the feet of mothers who trusted us to make our own entertainment, would strike out to find ponds and streams in which to dip our jars. Mischief was often afoot. We knew every abundant orchard within five miles and nothing tasted as fine as a scrumped apple chomped in the shade of a farmer's haystack.

Weapons were obligatory, of course. Pen-knives and catapults, feeble attempts at bows, blowpipes cut from hogweed stems. This was an age where the death of a sparrow or the pilfering of a pear tree were chastised but tolerated. Boys will be boys, the adults said. It's sad to think that only 40 years on, my own son can't enjoy such unfettered freedom. Political correctness and child abuse have cast a cloud upon such liberty. It's even more sad that today's youth don't even seek it, preferring the artificial world of cyberspace and gaming. But I digress.

Egg collecting
There was a hobby we had back then that is illegal now, and quite rightly so. In our innocence, we did not understand the concept of conservation and preservation. The competition to have the best birds egg collection was our equivalent of reaching

the highest level of a computer game. It took guile, cunning, knowledge and (looking back) unbelievable risk. When I recall swaying about in the uppermost boughs of a conifer being bombed by an irate sparrowhawk, it makes me shudder now. Lowering ourselves down the side of a flooded gravel pit to explore the sand martin nests? Climbing the interior of a dilapidated barn to reach the rafters where the barn owl nested? It took little courage, for we had no concept of fear. It did, though, take fieldcraft.

We learned how to identify every species of bird. How to sex them, their habits, their breeding season, where they would build their nests, how many broods they would raise. In essence, we were skilled hunters. Knowing your quarry intimately is the key to hunting. I don't look back proudly at the large collection I accumulated but I learned more about the birds I now either protect (and those I now legitimately hunt) than can be gleaned from reading a hundred books.

So now, in a perverse sort of reparation, I am highly equipped to preserve those species that most need help. Nowadays, as I did way back then, I still get a thrill listening to the yellowhammer's drawn call and the spar's chime. I still try to get a glimpse at the tuneful nightingale or try to locate the drumming woodpecker.

Protecting the songbird

So today I'm on patrol, in their defence, once more. Last month's attention to magpies was yet another mere skirmish in

Blackbird's nest

this constant war. Nature abhors a vacuum, as they say, and as fast as I can employ the rifle to reduce vermin numbers others will return to fill the void. I'm not complaining, mind you. It gives me the justification I need to be here. It's rewarding, though, to have the edge. Without doubt, as those kind farmers who allow me to play in their huge gardens can testify, my presence makes a slow, subtle difference. The knowledge I described above helps me to focus my preservation. Watching the robins, blackbirds, green woodpeckers, wrens, thrushes, blue tits and chaffinches prepare their nests was as enjoyable this year as in any year. They are all abundant species though. Nature will dictate their survival now that they're back in my wood or hedgerow, but I will continue to offer protection where I can.

If, like today, I see that yellowhammer and its mate taking material to the edge of the ditch or the greenfinches (so common in my youth, so rare here now) dragging moss into the hawthorn bush, I will be watching carefully on their behalf. I will attend the fragile gossamer ball that the long-tailed tits have woven in the reeds alongside the dyke. The sand martins are seldom seen today and their aerial skimming for gnats across the lagoon is sorely missed. I shall be watching for the rats which plunder far more from their burrows than my short, youthful arms ever could.

Close to all of this, a pair of carrion crows have taken up residence. An isolated oak, along a field's edge, is their choice.

The nest is complete; a spot where they can play sentinel and observe the comings and goings of both threat and food source.

The crow often refurbishes an old nest

So typical of the crow: perfect parent, predator, survivor and sage. They have my respect but not my protection! The ground level nest of the yellowhammers is at risk. They will have been watching the development with interest. The greenfinches have a better citadel in the hawthorn but the crow has a keen eye and a long beak. Those long-tailed tits are vulnerable too. I'm not equipped to deal with the crows today but, in my mind's eye, the plan is drawn up. I move on.

Another field, another farm, another problem. On most of the permissions I shoot over with an air rifle, game birds are forbidden, even 'in season'. None of them has a syndicate shoot in place but, understandably, wild game is a release for the farmer when he has time to enjoy with the shotgun. These gentlemen (and ladies) work hard, to a level it took me some time to appreciate. 24/7 is the modern term. My excursion on their land is functional, yet it is recreational. They rarely enjoy the same luxury. So, my role, is that of a surrogate gamekeeper.

What I do goes un-noticed and is tiny in terms of the grand scheme of the whole farm management but it makes me feel that I'm helping. In general terms, I make sure I do some housekeeping. Picking up litter and detritus, pulling the windfall branch away from the farm track, oiling a gate catch or hinge, shutting gates left open by – who knows? – reporting trespass. More often, challenging trespass, and not just by humans.

Plundered pheasant nest

I've had my eye on a wild pheasant's nest, in a ditch alongside a tarmac drive, for a while and thought I'd check its progress. It was a fortuitous decision. As I turned the corner of the hedgerow I was met by the sight of the hen bird racing up and down the top of the ditch where the nest lay, in an obvious state of alarm. When I reached the nest I found only four eggs left from a clutch of eleven. Close by, on the road side of the ditch, lay two more olive eggs. The ends had small punctures and the contents, still wet, had been all but drawn out. This wasn't the work of a grey squirrel, usually cowardly in the face of a plucky hen

pheasant. I crossed the track and just inside the wood I found another plundered shell, some yellow yolk still dripping from the aperture. I had just missed the perpetrator. I had a plan – a long-shot – and this would be a rare opportunity.

Fake rubber decoy eggs

I always carry my own clutch of chicken eggs at the bottom of my game bag; three rubber fakes bought from a toy shop years ago. I carved a section out of one and used fabric paints to make it look like an open shell showing white and yolk. I have taken out dozens of corvids using these little decoys.

I set this one, alone, at the edge of the track close to the pheasant's remaining brood and paced out 30 yards (my scope zero) to sit further up the track. I was banking on the almost predictable greed of the creature I had guessed had committed this crime. I waited for nearly an hour before

False hens eggs... realistic decoys

it returned. I saw its curious, nervous head pop up at the wood's edge, close to where it had left its last take-away. It bounced out onto the tarmac and I already had the scope aligned on the dummy egg.

Would it pass my decoy and flash straight into the ditch, or would it pause? The stoat, a cunning hunter in his own right, sprinted at the egg but jumped it and disappeared into the sedges. For a reason I will never know, perhaps my own sublim-inal instinct, I kept the gun trained on the egg. The stoat re-emerged and stole up to the rubber egg, pausing to sniff at the golden yolk. I didn't give it time to deter-mine its authenticity and the stoat rolled along the roadside under the impact of the pellet as the egg bounced toward me.

I sat back with a grin on my face. I've fooled squirrels this way before but never such a wily, fast-moving tyro as this mustelid.

As always, the initial surge of jubilation was soon replaced with a pang of regret. I

studied its lithe form and razor sharp teeth. In most instances, I would prefer to hide somewhere and watch a stoat – particu-larly when they frolic as a family unit. I rarely shoot them, but where I've felt it necessary (only ever when eggs or poults are their target) I usually bait with a fresh, dead rabbit. Their vampire-ish attack at the back of the neck of a coney holds them long enough for a shot.

With a single tiny pellet from an air rifle, you have no chance of catching them still at any other time. The wild pheasant now had at least a fragile chance of rearing a small brood.

Guns and ruses

Close to May 12th every year many countrymen and women will be digging in the attic for the old air rifle and drawing it from its oiled rags to take part in the local rook shoot. This is the time when the 'branchers', the hatchlings, venture from the nest and make their first attempts at testing their newly discovered wings. Swaying desperately on the boughs, high above the ground, it seems to me that the young rooks have enough to contend with in trying to learn the nuances of flight and balance without having to run the gauntlet of the gun. But this is the ideal opportunity to trim back a growing rookery and also a time for the air rifle shooter to prove they have mastered the difficult art of shooting

The pheasant's nest now had a chance

The clownish rook. Friend or foe?

elevations. The rook shooter, though, first needs to get past a moral dilemma forced on them by the mixed verdicts amongst country judges as to the pest status of the white-faced crow. Be it friend – or be it foe?

All about rooks

Most of the family *corvidae* are documented throughout folklore and associated across the ages with all manner of superstition and mythology . The rook is no exception. It definitely doesn't have the demonic demeanour of the crow or the raven. Most would say that its physical appearance (the white face and the baggy trousers) make it seem clownish. But never judge a book by its cover. The rook is an articulate and devious member of the crow family. Those who have watched a rook manoeuvre a road-kill rabbit to the relative safety of the central reservation on a motorway will know this. Or perhaps watched one drag a

fast-food bag from a bin and prise it open? Rooks are intelligent, opportunistic and very adaptable. Rooks are often credited with service to agriculture in the destruction of wire-worms and leatherjackets. Yet they can descend on drilled seed or on ripening crops with the same destructive impact as a flock of woodpigeon. They are included on the Natural England General Licenses for good reason.

The rookery itself is a marvellous spectacle for the naturalist. The 'ghetto' mentality of the rook is entertaining as they fight, fuss, squabble and steal twigs from each other's nests. At times they will line up along a nearby branch or wire, all 'buddies', and you can almost hear Cole Porter playing in the background. Then some will fly out *en masse* in search of food. Others remain as a rear guard at the nests. True to this 'ghetto' mentality, if a threat should appear, all hell will break loose. They soar around the threat and mob like an attacking fighter squadron in a communal effort to beat off the danger. This is a trait rooks carry into the field

Rooks are communal birds

when they're crop raiding and can be used to the hunters advantage.

If the young 'brancher' is a sadly vulnerable target, the adult rook has all the caution of its cousins, the magpie and the carrion crow. Feeding at some distance from the field's edge is a natural survival instinct. Any movement or threat (the glint of glass or metal, the pink face of a human) will alert them to danger. To shoot a mature rook with an air rifle takes an equal level of concentration and guile. That's what makes the adult rook, to my mind, a noble adversary. So I have various ruses that I employ against these corvids.

Most of these are basic and will be familiar to the seasoned shooter. Sometimes, though, you stumble across a different gambit, quite by chance. Recently I spotted a chance to bag a few adult rooks which was as 'seasonal' as the traditional

Mobbing rooks

'branch shooting' of youngsters. It also had a similar narrow window of opportunity. More on that later. Before that I was hunting my quarry using some old tried and tested tricks.

Mature rooks generally won't let you anywhere near them, so you need to encourage them to come to you. This is where the protective, mobbing instinct of the rook gives you some leverage. It is one of this bird's few weaknesses.

Decoy scene for corvids

Today I started my crusade with a decoy scene on a field about to be drilled with maize seed. I have a foam 'flier', which looks from a distance like a spread-eagled crow or rook. Laid out on the field it looked like a bird in distress. Near it I set a full bodied, flock-coated crow, wired to a fence post. At the far end of the maize field I noticed the tractor had arrived to start drilling the dry land. The freshly turned soil would attract a host of rooks, but they'd be far off – too far for a shot or two. I retired into deep cover at the edge of the wood to watch what was about to unfold. When the flock began to fly in and follow the tractor, I started a distress call using an off-the-shelf crow call.

Before long, the distant clamour gathered rapidly and the first black scouts wheeled over the decoys to check them out. They circled and the mobbing started. This frenzy and their natural calls drew in dozens more rooks curious to know what the commotion was about. From the wood

I could barely see my decoys but I knew from experience that it was unlikely the birds would land on the ground.

I held my attention on the tree-line at the wood's edge. I watched the rooks as they swooped over the wood waiting for the ones foolish enough to perch in the trees. Only a couple were misguided enough to drift in and land without an overhead pass. They paid dearly for this recklessness, their demise sparking more pandemonium above the canopy of the wood before the flock departed. Recovering the fallen birds, I noted the encroaching tractor and plough. I noticed something else too. It was time for a change of plan.

Following the plough

As the machine drew its steel harrow along, it turned up moist sub-soil, rich with worms and larvae. Dozens of rooks settled behind it in a feeding frenzy, leap-frogging each other to be first to the newly tilled loam. I was deep beneath the trees watching the furrows advance toward me as the tractor continued its laborious journey from one end of the field to the other. I mentally measured the width of the plough. I reckoned it was about 6 metres per cut. Within another couple of turns, the birds chasing the tractor would be within airgun range. I also figured that the nearer the ploughing got to the wood's edge, the more probable it was that the rooks would dare to sit and observe from the trees.

Back in the wood I settled down to reload the magazines for the HW100K and wait for the inevitable. As the line of the plough drew closer, several birds drifted into the trees, wheeling down to snatch a worm or grub and returning to perch. The

Like a wake descending on a buffet...

activity warmed up. So did the gun. The birds were confused, to say the least. Were they mobbing for the worms or for their fallen companions? As the tractor passed for the next-to-last sweep of the field, the rooks still fell in behind and a couple more fell to the gun, knocked into the furrows.

As the tractor made its final turn at the far end of the field, I collected the victims and cast them onto the soil before the machine returned. As the driver approached he saw the pile of black feathers, raised his thumb to me and within a minute or two the rooks were respectfully interred beneath the turned earth. Ashes to ashes, dust to dust.

Astonishingly, twenty yards behind the tractor the surviving rooks still followed, hungry and opportune, like a bereaved family at a wake descending on the buffet. And I'll remember that next season.

Pebbles and potatoes

Selective placement of a tiny pellet into the kill-zone of any quarry despatched with an air rifle relies on several factors. One is an acute understanding of the ballistics of that pellet. Knowing the flight path and expected point of impact of your chosen ammunition before it exits the gun, is critical. You can only achieve this if you practice constantly.

Another crucial factor is the ability to range-find, to know, at a glance, the distance from rifle to quarry. Sure, there are gizmo's and gadgets (even some telescopic sights) that can help you judge the range to your target, but let's be realistic here. When an animated, cautious creature like a magpie appears on a branch along the path I'm stalking, it won't wait for me to pull a state-of-the-art laser rangefinder from my pocket, measure the range, put the gadget away, sight up the gun – and shoot. Cloud cuckoo land! These gadgets have a place, such as in a hide or simply sitting ambushing rabbits. On these occasions you can accurately measure the distance to sitting quarry or to a point where you expect to shoot it.

The need to judge distance
Hunting with an air rifle involves hand-to-eye co-ordination. Therefore, learning to judge distance, instantly, is a pre-requisite to success. It doesn't matter what gun you choose, as long as you are familiar with that gun, its ammunition and its behaviour – and no-one else can help you with this.

I play the 'distance game' all the time. I don't need widgets. I don't even have to have a rifle in my hand to enjoy the game. I taught myself very quickly that, with most telescopic sights, true distance is immaterial. I worked out that my pace is roughly a yard, so I measure everything in paces.

When I zero my scope, I set a target up at 30 paces. I don't measure it with a tape, so everything I shoot at needs to be estimated by judging how many steps it would take to reach it. I then learnt how any scope reticule I employ, and its ladder of mil-dots or marks, relates to those paces.

I discovered something else too and it took many 'misses' before the penny dropped. Range is best estimated in short multiples. Perhaps I should explain.

A rabbit sitting out at dusk demands that you judge its distance before you shoot. The human eye is calibrated to estimate longer distances from a standing position. Don't believe me? Try it. Pick out a thistle head in poor light. Judge the distance in paces. Place your game-bag on the floor where you stand. Pace the distance to the thistle. Were you right? I hope so. Now, kneel down and look back at the bag. It will look further away. Imagine it was a rabbit. If you were kneeling when you lined up a shot on that dusk rabbit, you could easily have over-estimated the distance and that 30 yard coney was (in your mind) 35 or 40 yards. The shot went over the top and the rabbit bolted for cover. Yet you can't stand up to judge true range in a situation like that or the rabbit would bolt anyway.

Try a different method to judge range: a sense check. Focus on a point about 10 paces away, which doesn't have the same effect on your vision as a longer range. Fix the distance in your mind. Picture a 10 pace ruler. Then, mentally, roll that 10 yard ruler out to your quarry, end over end. Is it three rolls, four rolls? Somewhere in between? It helps, trust me. I also use this method on longer distance shots with the

FAC rifle, but I change the length of the ruler. From behind a net, where distance is always harder to judge anyway, I know my middle decoy pigeon is set at 30 paces from the hide. The corvid that lands further out to check my decoys: is it 50 yards, 60 yards? I look at that marker pigeon. I roll the 30 pace ruler in my mind. Is it twice as far. Less? More?

Pacing it out

But how do you learn to judge the length of the ruler, the ten paces, the thirty paces, in the first place? That's simple: you walk it. You're already doing it every day. You just don't realise that you're doing it, unless you're in the same 'hunting' mind-set as me. Everyday activity gives you the opportunity to play this distance game. It can even make for entertainment in some very boring situations. I hate walking my lurcher around the streets, on his leash. It's a labour of necessity at times but we'd both rather be un-leashed and in-country.

I use these opportunities, though, to reinforce the perception of range. How far is that second lamp-post? Judge it, then pace it. The Royal Mail letter-box? Pace it. That discarded Coke tin, the same size as a rat, imagine you've got the gun. Judge, pace it out, remember. Walking around a site at work on business. How far is that gate we're all approaching? Count the paces. Every innocuous exercise like this develops your mental 'range-finder'. Then, you simply apply it in the field; though you must test it there too.

In the field, there is often a very simple aid to judging distance which is overlooked by many shooters. The fence post. Farmers rarely set their posts randomly. They will be measured out (most on my farms are set 5 yards apart). Learn the measure on

A rabbit shot at exactly 25 yards. There are 5 yards between each fence post. I'm standing at the first

yours and use the posts to gauge distance to quarry. This is a very useful technique when stalking rabbit warrens.

Checking that my gun is zeroed correctly before every hunting trip is like a religious ritual. Dramatic shifts in zero are rare, but sometimes I need to tickle the scope turrets a tad to be perfect. Depending on my mood and also the proximity to

my intended hunting ground, zero checks can be either calculated (such as a plastic Pathfinder target or a metal spinner target at 30 paces) or random (a large pebble on a gatepost then pace 30 yards away).

There is an important and ergonomic difference though. The Pathfinder needs recovering after I've shattered it, as I won't litter my permission. The spinner needs retrieval for future use and has to be carried in my bag, but the pebble allows me to walk on and hunt, if the zero was true. Natural targets are always the better option and are so easy to find.

Natural practice targets

Throughout all of our seasons, natural targets abound: conkers, sweet chestnut kernels, stones, dandelion heads, thistle heads, bird feathers, all of which can be set up, shot at and abandoned. Only if you miss them, by a large margin, do you have a quandary. If you can't find zero, your gun so far off target that the scope needs a complete reset (and this can happen if you've knocked the gun heavily) you may need a broader backstop to see how far and in which direction the pellets are landing. High, low, left, right?

During the summer months, you may get away with a large broad leaf such as wild rhubarb or hogweed. In the winter, forget it: you need paper or cardboard. Back to the proverbial drawing board. A fallen, dead trunk can be used if you can find one but please don't use a living tree. The odd slug in a branch while hunting

The pebble, though, can be shot and left

is inevitable. To pepper an area of living bark simply to adjust a gun is poor form and won't please the tree's owner.

Two range-finding tests

So, with the gun zeroed, you need to test your range-finding skill and accuracy before you even consider shooting at vermin, because quarry will appear at haphazard distances when you move on to the real thing. If wild creatures all sat or perched along a 25, 30, 35 pace measure, hunting would be easy – and boring. They don't. So are you confident that you can judge a point between, say, 30 and 35 paces? Here are two small tests I recommend you take.

The first is the easiest. Take a pocketful of small potatoes (pigeon head size) into the wood. Sharpen some dead sticks and plant the potatoes into the ground in a line.

Three will do. Pace away to your guns zero range (25 or 30 paces, whichever you've chosen for your gun) and stand with your back to the targets, rifle loaded but un-cocked. Turn around and see how fast you can shoot each potato – it doesn't matter which rifle you have, PCP or springer. As fast as possible for *you*, that is.

You pass if you shoot each on its first shot because you clearly understand your gun and are taking the time you need to formulate the shot. You fail if you miss even one because these spuds aren't moving and can't escape. A live rabbit wouldn't allow you a second shot. If you shoot all three within 15 seconds, you are an extremely proficient PCP shooter and using a multi-shot rifle. If you shoot all three within 30 seconds with a spring powered gun, you know how to handle it well, how to reload it quickly and find target. It doesn't yet mean you're good enough to hunt. You need to pass the second test.

This second test is much more ambitious. Find an open area in either a wood or field. Take a couple of handfuls of spuds (about rabbit's head size), spin around and throw them out in all directions. Now, set about shooting them where they landed. Take as much time as you want on this test. This means that you will have to judge the range to each target. The 'rabbit heads' will be in random positions, some visible, others partially obscured by twigs, grass or foliage.

This is a much more realistic test of your shooting ability and mirrors a typical hunting situation. It's also far more fun than plinking away at paper targets or tin cans. How did you do?

Pathfinder targets

There is also a time, too, for static targets and markers in the hunting field. I use those little orange or yellow Pathfinder targets and always carry a few in my bag. Also in my bag will be a few coffee-stirrers, poached from fast-food outlets and coffee shops (I don't feel guilty, given the price of their bloody awful coffee). Why, though,

would I want these and the Pathfinders in my bag?

There are many times when this now-developed hunter's eye will be thrown out of perspective. Night shooting (lamping) is one such time. A few well-placed light-reflective Pathfinders along a warren can help you judge ranges. Working with colour filters on a gun-lamp again clouds your judgement. I'll often place a

*Shooting elevations –
practice, practice, practice*

The Pathfinder – a pocket sized, zeroing aid. But it needs to be recovered

When I use a leaf-net to ambush rabbits, squirrels or corvids I place the coffee-stirrers out at set distances: 20, 30, 40 and often 50 paces. If the distance to the quarry is suspect, these unobtrusive markers can be easily seen through the scope and they put my eye back on track. Unlike the Pathfinders they're free, expendable and, should I forget to pick any up, even bio-degradable.

Pathfinder in the ground behind me as I work a hedgerow at night. I'll walk up 30 paces, turn and quickly train the beam on the target. It implants a mental gauge on my brain.

When I hunt on and shine the red or orange beam on a rabbit's eye, I can now judge its range more easily. These targets can also be used to mark fallen quarry as you move along and therefore allow easy retrieval on the return trip, assuming you trust the fox not to steal that fallen quarry! Pathfinders are useful when judging distance in mist or fog too, which can be extremely deceptive.

Coffee-stirrers

Now, those stolen coffee-stirrers? Shooting from behind a net or from within a hide also deceives the eye and you can easily mis-judge range. This is less likely when you've set decoys, as you can place them at a 'paced' distance as described earlier.

Judging range on elevated targets

You will be hard-placed to set such targets or markers at the top of a tree, however. Judging range on elevated targets is a much more challenging prospect. This is a black art where the pellet is concerned but, again, practice will pay huge dividends. A respect for the laws of gravity is essential. Remember that Newton's Law comes in

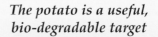

The potato is a useful, bio-degradable target

to play from the moment the pellet leaves the muzzle of your rifle. The horizontally-fired pellet, upon exit, rises for a while (unfettered by the confines of the barrel) and starts to fall as it loses speed. The elevated shot will be falling faster as it exits. Gravity pulls it downward, dramatically. So you aim as if shooting a nearer target.

As a general 'rule of thumb' I'll take 5 yards off for a 45-degree upward shot. So if the crow in the crown of a tree is 30 yards from my muzzle, straight line, I will be using the 25-yard mark on my scope's retical. That, dear reader, is simplifying the process unbelievably. You need to learn your own gun and your chosen pellet's behaviour on elevated shots.

How do you achieve this? Well, autumn's fruits give the best opportunity to practice elevated shooting: apples, pears, sweet chestnuts, conkers. Pine cones are available throughout most of the year and the Lord put them high up there for the hunter's education and entertainment, I'm convinced. Master knocking these fruits out of the boughs and you've taught yourself one of the blackest and most rewarding of all air rifle hunting arts. The aroma of woodpigeon breasts simmering in a winter casserole will reward any shooter who wondered why they spent so long peppering apples with lead on the trees during autumn.

The Old Hall

The searing heat of this late May weekend signals that we are on the cusp of summer. The sun is already high when I trundle the Jeep along the concrete drive to the Old Hall and cut a swathe through the hordes of winged insects dancing between the cream florets of the hogweed that line the track. In the cattle meadows on either side, rooks till at the hard earth and a pair of magpies leapfrog each other as they hunt bugs among the cow-pats. It's only been four months since I gained permission here and I've fallen in love with the estate.

I choose a shaded cleft beneath some tall conifers to park and, as quietly as I can, retrieve the rifle and the game-bag from the back. The resonant clunk of the tailgate

Ready for action

stirs a dozen woodpigeon from roost among the pines and they clatter away. Slipping on a camouflage gilet, I load the pockets with knife, pellet-magazines, mobile phone and car keys. The game-bag will carry little today: just my cameras and bass-bag. I top off with my baseball cap, for this sun will not only hamper my vision but also fry my receding pate. I snap a magazine into the rifle, flick on the safety catch and set out.

The dark, familiar silhouette of a grey squirrel

I have no particular design on any specific quarry in mind today. That's the beauty of the air rifle: its versatility. Sometimes a patrol is best left unplanned. Today I just want to amble slowly around the perimeter of this lovely estate and see what chances into my scope. So, which way first? As if in answer, a peacock calls down in the garden wood and I accept his invitation. I follow the steep path down alongside a crumbling flint wall which is slowly being torn asunder by the probing roots of the ivy which clings here. This makes a verdant fascia with numerous nooks and crannies, favoured by weasel, wren and robin. The pigeon continue to punctuate my walk, flashing from yew and larch above my head. At the

end of the wall is a gate, through which I slip silently to stand and let my eyes adjust to the gloom of the ornamental wood.

A movement to my left draws the eye and I watch the peacock slip over the wall and head back from whence I came, as if handing the guard duty to me. I stalk slowly from shadow to shadow under towering beech and larch. A stretch of broad, rust-coloured wings from a low bough surprises me and accentuates the darkness beneath this canopy. A tawny owl, abroad at ten in the morning! Her sweep through the trees sets off a chattering and hissing which sets me my first task of the day: grey squirrels. Padding cautiously in the direction of the noise, I crouch next to a trunk and scan the tree-tops. There are two or three youngsters chasing in the crowns, fast and elusive.

Then a scratching sound brings me to watch a larch trunk some fifteen yards off. Two squirrels, playing tag. One hooks onto the bark a few feet from the floor, sideways on to my gun. The shot knocks it from the trunk and as it rolls along the floor, I raise the muzzle to the tree-tops. The youngsters have frozen. I pick one, shoot and listen to the snap of the twig which saves its life. The others vanish. This corner of the wood is now in minor chaos. Pigeons have fled, some nearby jackdaws are protesting and the blackbirds are piping. I recover my squirrel, place it in the bag and move on.

Toward the far end of the garden wood I meet with a sad sight. A trail of huge

The squirrel looked out of place amid the blossom

tail feathers lead me to the spot where a fox has dined royally on one of my Lady's peacocks. There are wing feathers from a hen-pheasant here too. Old Charlie has been precocious and will surely pay for his sins. As I'm studying this, I notice the familiar dark silhouette of a grey sloping off along an oak bough. It's a little too near for my liking so I allow it to travel on. When it reaches a spot some twenty yards from my muzzle, I purse my lips and squeak. The shot is clean and the squirrel tumbles down through the rhododendrons, glorious in their May bloom. Another for the bag.

I leave the murk of the wood and step among the decorative trees that line the North Drive to the Hall. Cherry, apple, chestnut, hawthorn and lime, all resplendent in blossom. A single rabbit lopes across the lush, manicured turf. I shoot it and it looks strangely out of place lying dead amid the pink and white blossom petals. So, too, the squirrel that hops across the drive ten minutes later.

I move on again, this time along the edge of a cabbage crop and into the North Wood. I love this place; a mixture of ancient deciduous trees, magnificent Scots pines and younger plantation all stretched along a dog-legged escarpment. A single path cuts through its length, a path which I suspect has been walked by both keeper and poacher for centuries. Hundreds of woodpigeons roost here yet few are shot, their view giving them advantage over the approaching gun. As I shuffle in at one

The bag was filling fast

end, an ivy-tangled promontory, over fifty woodies exit, much to my frustration. So I settle behind an ivy hang for a while to see if any return. The short wait pays off when a lone pigeon drops onto the bare limb of a dead elm and lingers too long. The bag is filling.

Trudging up the slope toward the top of the escarpment (we're talking Norfolk here, so it's not exactly crampon and rope territory) I hear the alarm calls of several blackbirds. They haven't seen me yet, but this ganging-up of cock birds is familiar to me. It isn't the two roe deer which rise from cover and thunder off who are annoying these birds. I creep forward, half-watching the ground beneath my boots lest I step on a twig.

Over the rise, I halt and watch the path ahead. Among the nettles to my left I catch a fleeting glimpse of light red fur. Is it a cat? I stay still, as the blackbirds continue their barracking. I can see three cocks and their positions are tri-angulating the threat. The nettles move subtly toward the path and out she steps. A young vixen, not much bigger than a tabby but in rude health. She stands and glances in my direction, her dark ear tips twitching, her nose scenting the breeze but I'm downwind, in full camo, against a tree trunk.

The camera in my game-bag is screaming to be released but I know just one move will expose me. She licks her lips, making me wonder what mischief she's been up to, then slopes off into cover again, followed by her hecklers. Could she – such a small fox – have murdered the peacock?

Airguns for foxes?

Now there are a few FAC airgunners who would shoot a fox but I'm not one of them. A .22 pellet at high power, through the eye-socket and into the brain would almost certainly be terminal. But accurate though I may think I am, the level of certainty needed to dispatch such a large creature is too marginal to consider. Injury, perhaps even surviving with one eye blinded, would be reprehensible. Had I held a rimfire today, I would not hesitate if the backstop was sound. There are the tools for fox despatch but the air rifle (even at high-power) is not one of them. So I enjoyed the moment, watching one of our sharpest natural predators pass by.

Woodpigeon triumph

Further along the path and around the dog-leg I'm still losing the battle against the woodpigeons, which seem to be able to spot every shadow. Just about to emerge from a leafy section of the path into pines, I hear a pigeon murmur close by. I steal slowly out and look up to see the distinctive arse-end of my quarry overhanging a branch. The 'cooing' is still coming from the end I can't see. As if to add insult to injury, the bird lets go some squit which narrowly misses the end of my muzzle. I train the scope up onto the birds tail feathers, put my tongue in the roof of my mouth and imitate the 'chuck' of a squirrel.

Tails and feathers for the fly fisherman

Sure enough, the pigeon shuffles around on the branch into the line of the waiting rifle. The pellet, placed just above the crop, hit it before it could react to seeing me.

Further along again and another roe deer gets up from the side of the escarpment, running just a dozen strides then halting. She seems reluctant to leave, even stamping the ground and bobbing her head as if threatening me. Looking at where she rose, from among thick cover, I suspect she may have fawns nestled there so I hurry on. As I look back she still hovers above the cover, watching me but not running.

At the far end of the North Wood, as I'm about to walk out into the crops again, a hare rises almost beneath my feet and I very nearly drop the gun. It sprints out and stops amid a parched cabbage crop which is begging for rain. I watch the beast for a while - again, not airgun quarry - from the shade of the wood. When I step out into the open, the heat and humidity of early afternoon hits me like a fist. I realise I have a thirst that needs quenching.

On my way past the gardener's sheds I stop to trim the tails off the squirrels and leave them hanging in a plastic bag on a nail outside the door. The gardener, Ralph, says he wants them for a fly-fishing friend. I suspect, though, that our Ralph is just checking that the newcomer is getting results. No matter.

Turning toward the Jeep I see one of the peacocks on its roof. The same one as earlier? Who knows? He flutters down as I approach and screeches with disdain. Does he know how many pigeons evaded me? Does he know I didn't shoot his brother's assassin? I wave the full game-bag at him and thank him for the invitation. Up above the wood-turner's shed, on the topmost sprig of a sycamore, a stormcock puffs up its speckled chest and sings its weather forecast magnificently, but against the backdrop of a clear blue sky. Foolish bird.

A few hours later, as I sit on my garden deck scribbling these notes, the pigeon breasts lie in the freezer with the rabbit meat. The squirrels will find their way to a raptor sanctuary tomorrow. The swifts are circling beneath a bank of rolling thunderheads and the lurcher has slunk behind the sofa. The blackbird is high on the neighbour's cherry tree singing like that mistle-thrush earlier. My apology to him. I do hope it's a cracking, violent thunderstorm. It will round off a perfect day.

June

Rabbit Thief

The fox that stalks the rabbit sees the man,
The Hunter notes the fox and where it ran.
Who's hunting who, or what, becomes confused,
A crow observes the scene and seems amused.
The Hunter checks behind, from whence he's been,
To see Old Charlie creeping from the scene.
The rabbit... shot and left... has now departed,
And the hunter with the gun has been outsmarted.

A neglect of duty

The abundance of rabbits I'm seeing now is in contrast to the scarcity I witnessed in spring. As an outdoor type, I relished the sharp frosts and snowfall that characterise a hard British winter, and it had been some years since we'd enjoyed such a defined transition between both seasons. It was short-lived and still no comparison to those winters of my youth. Yet it definitely tempered the breeding activity within the warrens. An ambient climate (whether due to global warming or not is still a matter of speculation) just doesn't seem healthy for man or beast. The explosion in the rabbit population during those mild winters was a case in hand. I had shot kits in all months of the year. Not so this year. But now the coney's are making up for lost time. So too are the parasites which rely on the rabbit as

a host. That brief winter freeze cleansed the burrows of fleas and my spring harvest was relatively clean. Recent shooting expeditions, however, have seen them back with a vengeance. In the words of the immortal song – I can see trouble ahead!

Here in Norfolk I can't drive anywhere without seeing young rabbit kits by the roadside. They are everywhere: on the verges, central reservations, urban hedgerows, country lanes! Anyone conversant with myxomatosis will know that nature has a habit of controlling such surplus.

I worry that a couple of weeks of summer rain will push the rabbits underground for long periods. If 'myxie' takes hold now (and it no longer respects any season) there will be disaster for the rabbit shooter if all these kits and their parents are holed up in numbers. It will spread like wildfire: rabbit blood, to flea, to rabbit blood.

Evening rabbit shooting

This evening I raced from work, gathered together my kit and dashed to the sheep farm. I'd phoned the farmer to say I'd be over this evening. This is a shooter's nirvana of exposed, sandy warrens and woodside burrows. Unloading the gun in his yard, Jimmy came out to chastise me. 'I thought you'd forgotten about me! Bloody place is teeming with rabbits!' I felt a twinge of guilt at my inattentiveness but I was mindful that farmers and hyperbole can go hand in hand.

Shouldering the gamebag, I drew the HW100K from its slip, snapped in a full magazine, flipped up the scope covers and sidled around the lambing pens to scan the field. Bloody hell! There *were* rabbits everywhere! I had to blink a couple of times to get this into perspective. Now I definitely felt remiss. Jimmy hadn't exaggerated.

I crept back into the empty lambing pens. These give a view over the entire field from slits in the walls, reminiscent of those old wartime 'pillboxes' that dot this part of Anglia. I stared, still amazed, at the numbers of rabbits out feeding. There must have been over a hundred coneys browsing in the evening sunshine. And not just rabbits: there were magpies and jackdaws among them too, within gunshot. A magpie is always hard to resist but I had a more important commission tonight. My reconnaissance was disturbed at the flash of a swallow sweeping into the pen and landing on a low beam. The fledglings at the entrance of a nest above squealed and

clamoured for attention but the parent, seeing me, fled. I moved outside quickly, feeling intrusive. The parent would return soon to feed the chicks.

I tested the breeze. Which ever way I ventured it would disturb some browsers. I decided to head toward a small cluster of oak trees in the centre of the meadow. Even before I reached the shelter of the trees, some two hundred yards away, I had three in the bag with three shots. It promised to be a bountiful evening.

Settling behind one of the trunks, a glimpse of red fur caught my attention. Forty yards away, crouched amid a cluster of thistles in the open field, a rudely healthy dog-fox watched me cautiously. As I drew the camera from my bag he fled toward the copse at the bottom of the vale, leaving me with the sight of a disappearing brush. Surprisingly, the grazing rabbits through which he fled took scant notice of him. I reckoned his lush condition was down to this rich source of easily available protein. It was a shame he'd seen me: I would have enjoyed watching him stalking in such an arena. There was plenty of quarry here for both of us to share and the shooter can learn much from such a natural hunter. I took the precaution, though, of hocking and hanging my three rabbits, just in case Old Charlie crept around through the back fence while I progressed.

The shooting position among the trees posed a problem. I was having trouble sighting the rabbits grazing amongst the thistles and weeds. A brief squeak through

Rabbits, rabbits everywhere

pursed lips is enough to get a rabbit up on its haunches and into the scope. Using this method turned the thistle bed into a pop-up range and another four rabbits were bagged in reasonable time. The whisper-quiet snap of the silenced HW100K barely disturbed the browsers. The most condensed cluster of rabbits were out of range, near to where the fox had entered the wood. The only way down there was to follow the fox's audacious example and stride down through the rabbits. But they saw me as more of a threat than him! My saunter down put to ground everything within a hundred yards.

Tucking in close to an overhanging hawthorn bush, I waited for them to re-emerge. Letting nature settle down around me, I basked in the evening birdsong. The wood behind echoed to the rowdy squall of jays and the murmur of woodpigeon, two very conflicting sounds. A goldfinch bobbed onto the crown of a willow sapling and marked its dominion with the harsh '*zeezeeewit*' which belies its glamour.

Why do some of natures most colourful birds carry the most ugly tune? I digress. I enjoyed the opus, before unleashing the slaughter. To disturb such fragile tranquillity felt like casting a butterfly into the path of a hurricane.

Cull of baby rabbits

But with the light breeze now favouring me, the action started again. As usual, it was the gullible kits that ventured out first. Because there were so many, I culled these mercilessly. On a lightly populated warren I would have been less ruthless, preferring to farm them for the pot when they were mature. But the numbers here were of plague proportions so there was little option.

A young doe rabbit will multiply six-fold within five months. She will be fecund at four months old, deliver a brood of maybe half a dozen kits and will probably be mounted again on the day she gives birth. There can be no sentiment in pest control. I was on this farm for one reason, and it wasn't to film for *Springwatch*. Respect for quarry? Absolutely. Compassion? I'm afraid not. Once I have a rifle at my shoulder and a resolution in my mind, I have the same focus as my fellow hunter, the fox.

The magpie chattering in my pocket (my mobile phone's ringtone) alerted me to a message. It was time to head home for dinner, I was reminded by my hungry wife. Crossing the meadow to recover the fallen was akin to gathering up after a pigeon shoot. I retrieved the hat-trick I'd hung earlier and set about the chore of paunching.

This was a time to be selective. I had 18 rabbits of variable age and size: not bad for a few hours' work with an air rifle. The scent of rabbit paunch is a persistent odour which I prefer not to carry about me. I always carry a few of those plastic gloves deftly poached at petrol stations when I fill up with diesel. I also stash a small pack of antiseptic hand-wipes in my bag. This isn't 'dainty', its just sensible.

I chose eight rabbits as suitable, clean pot-fillers. I then squeezed the bladders, paunched out and packed them (not without a struggle) into my game bag. They would be hung overnight in the garden shed that my lovely wife refers to as 'the butcher's shop'. Normally, I'd take the kits too and hand them over to an acquaintance who runs a raptor sanctuary. As I wasn't likely to see her for some time, I left the unwanted rabbits hidden discreetly in a deep nettle bed for my furred and feathered hunting rivals to seek out and recycle. Despite my respect for Old Charlie and Mr Magpie, I took some gratification from the fact that, when they found them, they'd be licking stinging pads and claws for days in

This ain't Springwatch, folks!

payment. As someone once said; there's no such thing as a free lunch!

On the trek back to the Jeep, another adult rabbit bounced out onto the grass front of me. Shall I or shan't I? It was too good an opportunity to pass up so I took the shot, made more difficult with the game-bag pulling at my back. A clean headshot at just over just 35 paces. The rabbit was far too healthy to waste, so there was a delay while I 'gloved up', squeezed out and paunched again. The 'butcher's shop' would be busy tomorrow!

As I stepped into the house I was greeted by the aroma of a slightly burnt dinner. There was a glare on the face of my gorgeous wife. Oh dear! Butterflies and hurricanes?

As I said, there's no such thing as a free lunch.

Net profit

Very simply, pest control with an air rifle is achieved in one of two ways. You wait for the quarry to come to you – or you go after the quarry.

The latter is probably the more challenging method. Walking and stalking can be a total lottery. You carry your rifle and you take your chances, though those chances improve considerably as your field-craft skills develop.

Ambushing quarry from a hide is often more reliable for fast results. You know exactly what you intend to shoot and you can stack the odds with baits and decoys. Ambush hunters need a special attribute, one I confess I don't have in spadefuls. They need the patience of Job. Despite this, I often resort to calculated (rather than random) pest control. Sometimes there can be nothing more therapeutic than to set up in one of those areas on one of my shoots which I call a 'vermin crossroad', an area where I know from observation that several species may chance by. If my mood is right, it's a chance to recharge my batteries for a few hours, just sitting, listening and watching.

One convenient method of hiding up in the corner of wood or field is the leaf-net. Lightweight, easily erected using hide poles and no more of a burden than a sea-fishing rig. I use nets with modern, realistic photo-processed technology which duplicate the surrounding flora. I usually carry a pair of 5' x 10' blinds and four telescopic poles with kickplates (to drive them into hard terrain with my boot). The entire kit (and a tripod seat) fits into a quiver bag and carrying it over country is no major trial. It can be set up or dismantled in minutes which is handy if you need to relocate quickly. These modern nets are very deceptive. From the inside, they can seem very flimsy and give the user an impression that they are still exposed. From the other side your quarry has little chance of spotting you, provided you have set up against a solid, dark background.

This weekend's outings saw me using

the nets against two different problems on two separate farms. On one, the woodpigeons and rooks were plundering the new maize drillings. On the second, a very inapproachable rabbit warren needed some attention. The nets proved invaluable for both situations. Though I would use different tactics at different times of day.

Leaf-blind nets on edge of wood

Saturday morning saw me up before first light, loading the nets and decoys into the Jeep for that day's excursion. The leaf-blinds would be the main cover but were complimented by the backdrop of a small spinney next to the seeded maize ploughings. The spinney is a regular short-stop roost for both rooks and pigeons. On a recent drive around the field margin, my Jeep had turned the corner of the copse to be met by an eruption of black and grey from the rich, brown earth. Time for some action and I knew I had to be set up at first light to reap most benefit.

Time to paunch out

My primary target would be the pigeons, with their bulging crops and predatory nature. The picking and pecking of rooks will take as many grubs and beetles as it does seed. Shoot them I will, though often with reluctance. To sit at sunset watching legions of rooks drifting back from the fields is still, for me, one of life's rich pageants.

Setting up the decoy pattern

I set out a decoy pattern for the pigeons, spread around the feeding area but within range of my nets at between 25 and 40 paces. I also set a simple crow decoy scene close to the spinney. I believe the odd decoy crow, placed away from the pigeon shells, offers a sense of security to over-flying woodies. The presence of the far more wary crow can kid the pigeon that this a safe zone in which to feed. For the air rifle shooter, the pigeon needs to land to present a target. Anything to encourage this increases the odds.

The crow decoy adds more. The passing carrion crow will be curious too. Should they perch in the nearby trees, it can only add to the tally. My nets were set in an opening between an oak and an elm, where hawthorn and ivy were competing for the ground beneath. A good backstop but with a good view overhead and in front.

Zero the rifle

As always, I checked the rifle's zero before shooting. I wouldn't get a chance once the action started. My 50mm metal rabbit-head was pushed into the ground 30 paces into the spinney, also giving me a visual reference to my zero range. This gives important 'spacial awareness' when peering through a net. A few pellets directed at the red rabbit before settling down confirmed

Always set nets against a dark background

the integrity of my scope-to-muzzle accuracy.

I settled in behind the nets and poured a coffee, fidgety but observant. A green woodpecker, obvious by its bobbing flight across the open field, flashed around the copse noisily for a while. There were pigeon landing at the rear of the copse. I had the wind judged correctly, so I wasn't too worried. I was set up on the lee side of the wood, in a moderate breeze.

The action starts

Then the main flock started to circle around and dive into the spinney. A few birds dropped onto the decoy pattern but flew off quickly. I heard several crash noisily

Setting out a decoy pattern for pigeons

into the trees behind my position so I slowly changed my position to view the trees behind me.

As the woodies dropped in, I picked off targets among the boughs. Sometimes you can pick one off and the rest will fidget nervously, but not fly. The report of the shot, from my silenced HW100K, is fairly innocuous but at times, the thud of a bird hitting the floor will disperse the whole flock again. The first caused little panic as it landed on the carpet of greenery below. The next, though, crashed onto the hard, rabbit-delved bank underneath the roost with a thump. The sound of pigeon wings clattering through foliage erupted all over the spinney, damn it !! The fun wasn't over though. Throughout the morning, the

birds returned regularly, pulled in by the decoys, and the bag slowly filled.

Rabbit afternoon

The rabbit warren was the afternoon's task: a vast set of burrows along a dog-legged fence separating my farmers field from a commercially run, private wood. Though the wood's owner has declined me permission to shoot within, I am allowed to shoot rabbits on the margin and to cross the fence to recover shot or injured vermin.

This situation arose due to the now-defunct *Ground Pests Act 1954*, which required landowners to control rabbits, including their predation on neighbouring land, even if simply by erecting fencing, an expensive option on a long stretch of common boundary. Far cheaper to allow someone like me a modicum of control. Under normal circumstances (without that permission) it would illegal for me to fire across or through the fence. All shooters would be wise to remember this. To fire across a boundary into un-permitted land is 'armed trespass' and brings to bear heavy penalties if caught.

The recent removal of the Ground Pests Act (rarely invoked, even when rabbit damage was prolific, but certainly understood) has probably disadvantaged fencing contractors but given more opportunity to shooters! More farmers will need help with control in coming years. But be warned: remember my point about 'armed trespass' and get written permission to shoot across a boundary and to recover shot or wounded quarry.

The nets were set up late in the afternoon. As the sun dropped I let the countryside settle down and the rabbits, deep below me, to forget about the disturbance caused by stamping about and driving net-poles into the soil. The hay field I was protecting is a large dome and the breeze that follows the contours can easily deceive. Today, it was helping me. The zephyr billowed gently into my nets, carrying my scent back behind me.

As I sat waiting, I listened to the almost mystic *'chirrs and chucks'* of magpies deep in the wood. It is a sound they only make when off-guard and relaxed – a good sign. The drumming of a woodpecker added percussion to the shrill nagging of shrews below the blackthorns. A woodpigeon murmured with annoying confidence, somewhere within range but hidden by foliage. Peering voyeuristically through the net felt like looking through someone else's window.

A sudden movement made me look again. It was a grey squirrel foraging along the fence-line. It was tempting but I'd sat in wait for rabbits too long to advertise my presence. A flock of long-tailed tits appeared in the blackthorn boughs above me and trilled, scolding me. Sleepy now in the afternoon heat, I peeped out again and the adrenalin rush was instant. Sitting just 15 yards along the border was an adult rabbit, browsing nonchalantly. At that range the outcome was academic. It was my reason for being here. I sat back and waited for more to emerge, leaving the dead coney where it lay.

Slowly picking off rabbits as they emerged into the meadow was punctuated by watching the swifts sky-coursing midges above the meadow, like tiny avian greyhounds sprinting and jinking, snatching their quarry on the move. It was, as so often with the nets, a profitable day. Several rabbits would join the pigeon breasts in the freezer. The swifts, following the midges driven ground-ward by air pressure, presaged the approaching rainstorm. I stowed the nets in minutes, paunched out the rabbits and trekked back to the Jeep with my booty.

Magpies and mafia

Driving along a narrow lane I noticed a commotion on the road up ahead. Two adult shelducks were trotting up the lane and a pair of magpies were diving in and out of the bushes, appearing to attack the ducks. As I got nearer I could see two tiny ducklings between the adults. Each time the magpies flew in (alternating their attacks), the parent ducks rounded on them, successfully repelling the assailants. This was an allied infantry platoon against an enemy aerial squadron.

They needed heavy artillery, so I edged up in the Jeep, close enough to intimidate the raiders who veered away and left the scene. I followed the duck family slowly down the lane until they herded their young into cover. I drove off wondering how many of the brood had already been plundered by the magpie pair?

Shelducks would normally rear about a dozen chicks. There was no sign of others about. That's why, ladies and gentlemen,

A successful afternoon's bag from behind the net

I get angry when I read claims by bird protection agencies such as the RSPB that magpies have no significant impact on chick predation. The adult shelduck is twice the size of even a large songbird. What chance does your average songbird parent have of protecting their brood?

Songbird massacres by corvids

In my own garden, I have had to endure the destruction of blackbird broods over two successive years by corvids: once by magpies, the second by a carrion crow. How can Ian Barnett (I sense you ask) with an array of air rifles at his disposal, allow such a thing to happen? Quite simply, the nests have always been on the periphery of my garden and I have neighbours to consider. Even when I've seen the beggars hovering near-by, waiting for an opportunity, I couldn't risk pellets flying over my boundary. Believe me, I've been sorely tempted to pot magpies and crows from the bedroom windows to allow a backstop but it's just not worth the risk of being 'reported', particularly as an FAC holder.

Over many years in the field I have been witness to innumerable acts of intimidation and infanticide by the 'Mafiosi corvidae'. I've also found enough post-trauma evidence to point the finger reliably at corvids as the perpetrators of a crime.
- The discarded magpie feather snagged in the blackthorn where the thrush nested.
- The long triangular imprint of a crow's beak in the broken shell of the blackbird's egg.
- The imprints of the crow's feet in the mud close to the pheasant's empty nest.

I have frequently seen (even photographed) the carrion crow or magpie passing by in spring with some unfortunate, pathetic, pink chick in its bill. Quite often I have been able to prevent a crime through observation and timely intervention with a pellet.

The jay

The jay is a handsome crow but don't let that attractive exterior fool you into thinking that it doesn't have the traits of its cousins. I've proved this to myself many times. Though it seldom comes in to feast on carrion (such as the gutted rabbits I use to draw in magpies) it rarely resists my decoy rubber eggs. If it will try to raid what it thinks are hens' eggs, you can rest

Songbird-attacking claws

assured that it will plunder the smaller eggs of its neighbours too.

The rook

The rook is viewed with leniency by some shooters but is high on the 'hit list' for others. It is on the General License for good reason. Perhaps not as a songbird predator (though it will take eggs if pressed by hardship) but more for its capacity to raid crops. The sheer number of rooks on agricultural land make it as much a threat as the woodpigeon on some crops. Yet it also gives benefit at times. When fresh earth is tilled, you will see this clownish corvid alight in droves to feast on leath-erjackets and other grubs exposed by the plough. These are larvae which will wreak havoc on a burgeoning crop. I suppose we could view the rook as 'cost-neutral' but please remember that the farmer will spray to eliminate insect pests. He or she can't spray to eliminate rooks. I have to confess, though, that one of the most magnificent natural exhibitions during an evening's mooch with the rifle is to sit back in awe and watch hundreds of rooks beating their way back from the fields to roost. It is a quintessential British spectacle.

The jackdaw

Where you see rooks, you will see jackdaws too. The two species seem to enjoy each other's company. The wheeling, diving aerial hi-jinks of the 'jake' contrasts with the slow, lumbering flight of the rook. Noisy, acrobatic and often amusing to watch, jackdaws too are on the General License. I have farmers who prefer me to leave these small corvids alone and I have others who insist that I shoot them.

The main crimes which call for control are their annoying habit of nesting in chimneys and blocking the flue (not that there are many chimneys nowadays) or roosting in the farm buildings. Just as with feral pigeons, the jackdaw roost can cause pollution and damage to animal feeds and grain stores through the depositing of guano where it is least appreciated.

The magpie

For me, the magpie is the corvid highest on the shooting A-list and is also the most challenging. Like the grey squirrel, it enjoys the mis-placed affection of the general public. Both species enjoy the sanctuary of gardens and parks. From there, they spread like a recurrent virus into the places where you and I seek to eliminate them.

The magpie, with its gift of flight, has a refuge rarely survived by the grey squirrel: the public highway. On a recent drive from Norwich to Cambridge, my son and I counted around 160 magpies on or near the road. This, within less than a two hour trip. Unwittingly, we feed them with our cars. They thrive on a ready-meal diet of fresh roadkill. Rabbits, pheasants, hedge-hogs and even deer are flattened daily for their delectation. Nesting and roosting in the no-go, no-shooting areas owned by Local Authorities and the Highways Agency, it's no wonder they keep coming

Rooks returning to roost – an awesome spectacle

back into the countryside to fill the territorial voids we create with the gun and the Larsen trap. We are losing the war of attrition against the magpie, dear reader.

Though it may appear otherwise, I love all wildlife, including corvids. You have to admire their skill as kidnappers and thieves. Their ability to work as a team is impressive. Their own sense of family value, even if selfish, is admirable and is why I describe them as a 'mafia'. It's not their fault that self preservation is in their genes. Yet, no-one should deny the need for a controlling force to protect the vulnerable from those who would exploit them. That task falls to the shooter or trapper.

A blackbird pair favoured us with a nest in the honeysuckle last month. I was driven to do my best to play sentry and try to help them bring on a brood. We rarely get magpies or crows near the bird feeders, but they do drift by occasionally. One day, when the hen was off the nest taking food, I counted the eggs. A lone egg in the nest indicated predation, yet I hadn't seen any

corvids about the garden for weeks. On Saturday morning, as I prepared my gear for a sortie at rabbits, the cock blackbird's alarm call rallied me in time to watch him aggressively chasing starlings from the bird table. With no sign of the hen, I checked the nest again. It was empty, with no sign of a broken shell in the vicinity. I couldn't believe that the starlings could be the culprits. Puckish as they are, I've never had them down as egg thieves. I reasoned it must have been a dawn corvid raid. Yet later, in the afternoon, I caught two starlings checking out the nest with what looked like malevolent intent. A bad Karma moment. So, the nest was deserted and we will see no young blackbird fledglings on the fence, testing their wings for flight, this year. In a fit of pique, I took the fat-balls off the feeders (so attractive to the 'wheezers', as starlings are known locally) and decided it was a case of 'guilty until proved innocent'. A few days later, I

Britain's little vulture clears the roadkills

photographed a carrion crow making an early morning raid on the bird table. The fat-balls were returned.

A crow in my garden – was it him or the starlings?

Species day

I have set myself a personal challenge; a target I doubt I will ever achieve in my lifetime. What is life without goals? This Herculean task isn't one which can be planned and schemed. It relies far too much on opportunity and sheer luck and we all know that luck is a lady long courted and rarely conquered. So it is with my unusual quest.

The air rifle hunter has limited quarry to pursue, within the confines of the General License and the Wildlife Act (or rather, the exclusions and exemptions from the Act). The target, the quest, the challenge, is permissible: to bag, within 24 hours, eleven different species allowed under the law. It ignores those species that are random or rare, such as mink, stoat, allowable gulls (probably now removed from the License). It ignores the easy moorhen, whose presence on the License makes no sense in the absence of the starling.

The challenge list is rabbit, rat, squirrel, magpie, jay, jackdaw, rook, carrion crow, wood pigeon, feral pigeon and collared dove. All abundant on my Norfolk hunting grounds, yet all so elusive when needed. Perhaps the hardest to nail under pressure would be the jay, and the carrion crow. Though the nearest I have got to achieving this is to bag all but the crow and rook. There have been many weeks when I've shot all on the list but the 24 hour challenge is the goal.

It is such an obsession now that, if a jay has fallen to the gun, you can guess the wife won't see me for a while!

The factor that makes it hard to achieve is 'Sods Law'. On the occasion when I needed crow and rook, nothing came down to my staked-out, gutted rabbit but more magpies. When you need a rabbit at the last minute, the fox comes creeping along the warrens. When you decoy for pigeons, the harvester turns in a different field and draws them away. When you target a jay with some eggs laid out in a fake nest, the crow comes raiding. And so it goes on. You can't plan it. It's simply all about walkabout shooting and suddenly realising that you are only a few species off target. That's when the adrenalin kicks in.

I've had days when I've shot rabbit, rat, rook, squirrel, woodpigeon, jackdaw, feral pigeon, but couldn't connect with the others. I've had times when I've taken the harder ones like carrion crow, magpie and jay in one session so have moved on to get squirrel, woodpigeon and feral pigeon only to find not hind nor hair of the staple quarry like rabbit or rat!

I've come to the conclusion that I may never achieve this in my lifetime – but what's a man without a goal?

I've had days when I've shot several on the list

One species down – ten to go!

July

Summer Storm

Beneath the grey and threatening, thunderous sky
The swifts cavort and pigeons hurriedly fly.
The Hunter sits in awe within the wood
To watch the storm's approach, and draws his hood.
The lightning's flashing fork precedes the sound
Of thunder-crack and pattering on the ground.
Amid a cloud of midge and humid swelter
The Hunter waits for quarry seeking shelter.

Swifts and storm clouds

It was the small squadron of swifts, hawking insects some twenty feet above the maize, that confirmed what the barometer in my head was telling me. These aerial acrobats are normally high-fliers and take their food up in the thermals. Track their flight and you are tracking the weather front. When they descend to feed this low, they are following the insects driven down under conflicting pressure fronts and you can hang your hat on an approaching storm.

Quiet July
July is perhaps one of the leanest months of the year for the air rifle hunter. Nesting is all but over, the second broods of many species are fledged. Squirrels are docile and harder to spot in the wood's leafy canopy. Rats have left the farmyard long ago, to forage in field, ditch or hedgerow. Woodpigeon, like the squirrels, enjoy the sanctuary of leaf cover. Even that perennial quarry, the rabbit, has high cover to protect it. Yet there are still many opportunities open to the walkabout shooter. A thunderstorm presents one of them.

This afternoon I've been sweltering behind a leaf-net, staking out the grass ride, a lush border around the growing maize. I've not seen a single rabbit exit, nor squirrel enter. The fallow herd has kept me amused, slipping silently 'twixt crop and wood. Even my avian friends have deserted me on this sultry, humid afternoon. The legion of midges plaguing my position swirl around and add to the chaos in my throbbing head. I often get a headache before a storm, which will dissipate as soon as it passes. I stripped down

Watching the storm front approach

Glancing up through the leaves there is a contrast of lush green against the gun-metal grey of the sky and the first distant roll of Odin's drum adds rhythm to the bird-song. Suddenly, dramatically, the woods fall silent.

Pulling on the camo rain-top, I check my gun. Today I have the company of my FAC-rated Weihrauch as I want to push the range a bit. Magazine loaded, safety catch on. My head is still pounding and I hear the approaching rain. The torrent of heavy water droplets drumming against the upper canopy sweeps toward me like a tsunami. Inevitable. Unstoppable. I brace myself for the drenching but, as it washes overhead, I barely feel anything underneath this vast umbrella of a tree. I'm crouched here because I know that rabbits and squirrels detest a soaking and I know there are dozens of them deep within this eight-acre crop. I'm here because I know that woodpigeon will flee the deluge and seek cover

the nets and packed them into the Jeep, parking it a few hundred yards away and out of sight of my hunting position. Then I stuffed some light rain-wear into my game-bag and crept back to the edge of the wood to await the storm.

Approaching storm

The dark thunderheads boiling, rolling against the blue sky, are gathering pace and as I settle into position, the swifts have disappeared. A cock blackbird has been trilling his eloquent storm-song high up in the copse, head-chorister to a burst of harmony from within the wood, Robin, chaffinch, willow-warbler, all join the choir. I have set myself under a huge and ancient beech, its broad canopy the best shelter in any forest, with a view along the same ride where I had placed my nets.

*Wrapped against the storm,
I watched the field margin*

in the wood. I'm here because I love the primeval sensation of a summer storm.

Drama in the storm

A rabbit lopes out first, twenty yards away, to pause at the edge of the maize. An easy shot made more challenging by the misting of my scope, but a kill nonetheless and marked vividly by a flash of lightning. I count to ten and the rumble of thunder tells me the storm centre is still two miles off and approaching. Another rabbit, too fast for me, sprints into the wood. A flight of woodpigeon, perhaps half a dozen, clatter in from across the tips of the crop. I can see two. One flashes off its bough as I raise the gun but the other lingers and falls to a pellet. A grey squirrel scampers to the fence-line beneath the beating rain. It bolts for a beech trunk thirty yards off and glues itself to the bark, a foot from the ground. The pellet, between the shoulder blades, releases its grip as it drops. The deluge increases in intensity and I'm getting showered now. I pull the hood of my cagoule over the baseball cap and tuck the rifle under the body of the rainproof to protect both scope and action.

A bright fork of lightning, followed almost immediately by the thunder-crack, sends a shiver down my spine. Bent beneath the tree I watch this most natural of spectacles pass, with awe. Flash, crack, flash, crack, until it passes. Between each boom the wood's silence is broken only by the patter of rain. No song, no flight, no movement, nothing. The wild creatures of the copse cower nervously under Odin's outstretched hand.

The rain stops as suddenly as it had arrived. I am damp but not sodden and the gun barely touched. The beech tree, as always, has served me well. Do I fear squatting beneath a tree in a storm, contrary to so much advice? No more than I fear getting into my Jeep to drive to work each day. If the gods dictate that my days should end beneath this tree, watching such a natural drama, then I concur with their decision. Far better that, than to end in an ugly tangle of metal and rubber on some distant motorway.

Valkyrie – my FAC HW100K

After a few minutes of un-earthly silence, the blackbird strikes up his song again, rallying forth the residents of the copse. Other song breaks out and movement starts up all around me, a celebration of survival. What do these beasts feel at the onset of a storm? What awe? I collect the rabbit and the pigeon and return to the Jeep to towel down my gun. I named this Teutonic gun *Val*, short for *Valkyrie,* the mythical hand-maidens of Odin who escorted the souls of the slain to Valhalla.

Perhaps, today, he remembered this, too?

Watchman at the water

Though not born here, I live in a county blessed with some of the richest agricultural heritage on mainland Britain. It is a naturalist's heaven and a rich hunting ground for those, like me, with a burning desire to shoot and also to record all those fauna we act to protect. There is a substance, a nectar, an essential element upon which every living creature depends and I am surrounded by it here. Water. The rivers, broads, lakes and ponds, even the sea, are never far away in this area. For the photographer they combine to offer a huge opportunity to observe wildlife. For the hunter, there are limits, for much of this area is restricted to the gun. Had I been born here, I may (like my father-in-law) have been tempted onto the estuaries and mudflats in pursuit of wildfowl.

I grew up mesmerised by the prose and evocative description of dark, wild nights and dawns on the foreshore described by that iconic writer, BB. My own father-in-law (Derrick Bailey) and his own father before him, enjoyed many such outings. His tale of being trapped in the deep mud off Breydon Water, in the dark, with the tide turning fast, makes my spine tingle. More so because he was on crutches, his leg in plaster and obsessed enough to need to get out and shoot alone. They say a fool and his money are easily parted. Not so a fool and his gun. But he survived and I'm sure that Derrick will forgive me that comment, for he knows that I have that same obsession. I understand what drove him out there that night. I'm sure that most readers of this book would understand too.

A visiting cormorant

The lure of water

Rivers, water courses, ponds, pools, puddles and splashes offer great opportunity to the air rifle hunter. So, too, do drinking stations: cattle feeders, troughs, bird baths. Staking out a river, stream or pond can be an enriching experience: not just in shooting terms but from simply watching the myriad creatures that pass by. The vivid azure flash of the kingfisher, the ploughed 'v' of the otter's nose on the water's surface, the heron's vigil at the rivers edge, the swallow dipping the surface with light splashes and the plundering cormorant.

Corvids and water

Corvids rarely stop over at the trough or splash-pool but occasionally they do.

Magpies at a water splash

Usually they're after the insects like midges or gnats that hover around these places. A favourite with the magpie is the pond-skater and while it's fishing around, it's a very vulnerable target. The woodpigeon is a regular drinker which is not surprising given its eating habits – a bulging crop surely benefits from a draught to help with the metabolism.

Mink and water

Another unwelcome visitor is the mink, though I confess I've never shot one. I've had fleeting glimpses of this alien mustelid but never long enough to train a scope on one, nor even photograph one. In my area, though, I have heard tales of plundered wildfowl collections and chicken coops, attributed to this pest. More efficient control is trapping and I often see mink-rafts placed in the dykes of marshland

Britain's largest avian predator, the heron

122

where I walk. These are conservation areas, out of bounds for the gun. Yet I've never seen an inhabited trap.

Rabbits and water

Rabbits tend to avoid water, but they do drink. You need to check the puddles formed in base of broad-leafed plants like rhubarb or twayblade. Where they are close to the warren, you will find rabbits taking a drink occasionally. Similarly, look out for the puddles left in the cleft of the beech after rainfall and you will find where the grey squirrel sups.

Rats and water

The most common vermin found at the watering place is the brown rat and this is reason alone to watch the farm troughs. The leptospires it carries in its urine survive in and pollute static water sources. A rather frightening fact is that around 70% of cattle

The cleft of a beech – a squirrel drinker

herds in the UK carry leptospirosis. An infected cow has about half the chance of conceiving young as a healthy beast. The disease, while relatively harmless to these large beasts, causes infertility.

Advice for shooting near water

A decent pop-up hide or good cover is useful when targeting water courses but is best set up for some time. Your quarry is used to visiting its drinking place and will be cautious if it spots something out of the ordinary. There are other precautions to take too, mostly common-sense ones. Water may mean mosquitos so use an insect repellent on exposed skin. Shoot carefully around troughs not just to avoid ricochets and potential injury to stock, but also to avoid puncturing troughs or pipes.

Shoot carefully around troughs – don't puncture them!

If you're shooting rats, take protective gloves and remove any shot ones without direct skin contact. Weil's Disease is a killer and a dead rat can wreak its revenge on the unwary shooter who doesn't observe simple hygiene rules.

The only good rat – a dead one

Perhaps the last piece of obvious advice here is: don't over-shoot watering places. Your quarry may abandon them for good.

The sheep farm

One of my hunting Nirvanas is a tiny hobby-farm buried amid one of Norwich's suburban outreaches. Simon Whitehead, the noted ferreter and writer, tipped me the wink on this place a few years back after Jimmy, the owner, had approached Simon for help at a game-fair. Norfolk isn't noted for its valleys but this 30-acre estate sits in a lush vale and looks, for all the world, like a corner of Cornwall. Jimmy, a retired grain merchant, keeps a small flock of sheep in the valley.

The first time I drove up to take a look and to meet Jimmy, he walked me out around the sheep pens and I stood mouth-agape, staring at the biggest concentration of rabbits (grazing out in the spring sunshine) that I had ever seen in such a small area.

As the spread of the city has gradually approached this land it has brought with it the problems that are typical when suburbia meets country. Along one side of the farm there sits a mobile-home park, occupied

Grey Wagtail at a pool – another treat while watching with the gun

mainly by retired pensioners. The southern edge is bordered by a large wood which has no designated public footpaths but has become an area of permissive access for dog walkers and a haven for local youngsters.

The pressure of disruption on the warrens has forced the rabbits on both borders to burrow right out into the sheep pasture. The proximity of the public and their dogs obviously makes it too dangerous and disruptive to use shotgun

An abundant open, sandy warren

control, so pest control had lapsed. Which is why Jimmy wanted a quieter solution such as the ferret or the airgun.

Over the past few years I have made a reasonable impact on the coney population. But I've never set out to obliterate the warrens. I just like being on the farm too much! Jimmy, I'm sure, will forgive me for admitting that I have farmed the rabbits to a certain extent, just to maintain access and good sport. Lamping would have taken a serious toll and though I made a passing attempt at lamping the meadows over two winters, I always met with unexpected problems.

Tact required when lamping

One dark evening, at the edge of the big wood, I almost tripped over two young lovers who had picked some derelict sheep-pens for an amorous encounter. They bolted, semi-clad and embarrassed, leaving me worried about just how close I'd been to them with a loaded rifle.

On another lamping trip it became obvious that (with winter's lack of foliage on the hedges) the sweep of my gun-lamp was disturbing the OAPs in their bungalows, the bright beam often ranging in their direction.

On yet another trip, my red beam picked up the reflections from an Alsatian's eyes as it stood growling at me, mercifully called away by its owner from within the wood. Why on earth they were walking the dog in the wood on a dark, drizzly winter's night (there was no sign of torch-light) I'll never know. Had it been a police dog, the officer would surely have come over to check what I was up to. As a result, though I still lamp occasionally, it is with a degree of reluctance on this land.

Gentle rabbit control

So, although Jimmy had high expectations of me culling hundreds of rabbits in a short time, I've resorted to a control regime, done by degrees and generally during daylight hours. When I first ventured here, the feeding rabbits would just continue browsing as their kindred were bowled over only yards away. Now, they're more gun-shy and many go to ground when one of their number gets shot.

Today I chose a late afternoon sortie using a leaf-net and poles to break up my outline. I knew the rabbits would be out to make the most of the warm sunshine after previous days of rain, so I wandered down to pick an ambush position.

As I appeared from behind the sheep pens, there were about 40 rabbits already grazing on the open, sandy warren. I was in no position to start stalking and shooting, due to the kit I was carrying. So, as I often need to do here, I just trekked straight through them and saw a cascade of white scuts disappear into the burrows which are destroying the sheep meadow. Frustrating – but they'd be back out soon enough.

Selecting a spot along the edge of the big wood which gave me a panoramic view of the open burrows, I set up the nets. There is a light breeze that pushes along this vale almost all of the time but this would only test my skill marginally if shooting across it. The nets were up within minutes and all my kit was stashed behind. I pegged the bottoms to stop the nets billowing – a sure giveaway – and set off to mark out ranges with some wooden coffee-stirrers. I set a few markers among the rabbit-holes around the hide at 30, 40 and 50 yards. These make for quick, accurate judgement of quarry distance, which is useful from behind nets.

Peering through camo-netting gives an increasingly false impression of distance, often making your quarry appear closer than it really is. This can result in over-shooting and nothing annoys me more than a rabbit going to ground with a pierced ear!

Pause for rabbits to return

All this activity and the vibration above ground, of course, would mean the rabbits sitting tight for a while yet. I lifted the rifle and a game-bag to take a stealthy walk around the top of the meadow. As normal there were a number of first-year rabbits browsing up here – too naïve to appre-ciate the danger of feeding out in broad daylight and not yet gun-wary. Cull such youngsters when numbers are high. Kits will soon mature into breeding adults and the fecundity of the rabbit is legendary.

I'm here to do a job and I clinically picked off a few with the near-silent Weihrauch to help fill the game-bag. These weren't mature enough yet for the table, but they would make excellent magpie bait over the coming weeks, stored in the freezer, then thawed when needed.

Soon I had crept silently back behind the nets to wait for the warren to come alive again. As the sun dropped, the rabbits would venture out again. I used the time to photograph bird-life: the bearded tits mobbing in the oak above me. A jenny-wren's angry feints told me I was too close to her second clutch of the year for her comfort. A few rabbits crept out, staying too close to the burrows for me to venture a shot so I was content to capture them on camera, waiting for the confidence of the warren to slowly build again. It didn't take long.

The action begins

Two simple targets presented themselves. One hopped out of the wood along the fence-line, 15 yards away and was flipped over. The second, at 25 yards, browsed just outside its burrow so I waited for it to hop a little further away before culling it with a .22 Rangemaster. By now there were numerous other rabbits feeding out, but way out of range at 70 or 80 yards away.

As they do, a couple of those distant rabbits started to flirt and chase, running within range but they were too near the OAP bungalows for a safe shot. One of these ventured into the field and started to browse within 40 yards of my muzzle but

out in the breeze which was cutting across my line of fire.

Judging windage is a practised skill and even the slight bend of the meadow grass gives clues. Add to that the refinements of modern rifle scopes (I use a Hawke SR6, with a superb reticule), wind-cutting pellets like the Rangemaster and such shots have minimal risk factor. I bowled the rabbit over and it laid, white belly showing, on the grass.

Local on-lookers

Another movement caught the corner of my eye and I suddenly became aware that I had an unexpected audience. There were two old fellers beyond the fence, by the OAP bungalows (some 50 yards west of the dead rabbit), hopping up and down and waving their arms at each other. Whoops! I did a quick mental replay. Had I shot in their direction? No. Could there have been a ricochet? No.

With three dead rabbits on the meadow and most of the others now underground, I decided I'd better retrieve the corpses in case they were upsetting the two old guys. I stomped out boldly to the last victim, pretending I hadn't seen the audience. I collected the other two rabbits, aware of the eyes boring into my back. Back behind the net, I hoped the two old boys would lose interest but they were now waving arms around, shouting and were on the upwind side of the warrens. I hadn't put the rabbits to ground with my shooting, it was these chaps! They obviously weren't going to go away so, shouldering the gun (magazine removed and safety-catch on) I wandered over to the hedge. They both stood with their arms crossed as I walked up. Now I do body-language in the day job. This didn't look good.

'Afternoon chaps,' I offered, 'I do hope I'm not causing you any concern? I do have permission to be here.'

As it turned out, I was way off mark. One of the guys had been watching the rabbit feeding just before I shot it. He's seen it jump two foot in the air then flop dead! He had then spotted the nets and called to his neighbour, who was washing his car. Though they'd figured out what had happened, they couldn't understand why they hadn't heard a shot. They fired a load of questions at me. What sort of gun is that? How far does it shoot? Why is it so quiet? Do you eat the rabbits? I answered all their questions, loaded the magazine

The kits would serve as corvid bait

and fired off a few rounds to demonstrate its silence, took the opportunity to explain it was my gun lamp they sometimes saw at night, offered them a regular supply of fresh rabbit (which they declined) and I went back to the nets.

Of course, it got worse. I was now a source of free entertainment. I spotted them both leaping up and down, waving to me in the hide and pointing wildly to my left. There, a brace of rabbits stood alert, 60+ yards away from my nets, way out of range and with a bungalow beyond. The rabbits dived for cover and my new fan-club (obviously disgusted at my reluctance to shoot) eventually got bored and disappeared indoors, probably to get their cameras! I took the chance to pack up and disappear. I paunched the 'pot-fillers' before leaving and left the offal discreetly at the wood's edge for the vixen to clean up.

Paunching out. The foxes will clean up later

Fur 'n' feather kebabs

Our kebabs always add a bit of spice to a family barbecue. Young Sam in particular relishes preparing these and is usually first in the queue when we're ready to dish up. Although there's a bit of primary preparation to do, they're worth the effort. During the spring and summer months, when I prepare rabbits for the freezer, I always make up a few bagfuls of boned and cubed prime meat taken from the saddles and haunches. I do the same with pigeon breasts. A bit of effort put in at that stage pays back when it's warm enough to fire up the barbeque. You just need to remember to defrost the meat in the fridge overnight.

Ingredients

Saddle and haunches of 2 or 3 adult rabbits, boned and cubed.
Half a dozen woodpigeon breasts, cubed.
One cold tin of Stella Artois
Two red onions
Cherry tomatoes
Mixed sweet peppers
Mushrooms
Smokey barbecue marinade sauce
Two bottles of Sangria

Preparation

Most importantly, pour the chilled Stella Artois into a glass and take a large draught. Dehydration is a terrible thing and is not conducive to good cooking. Next, having checked that the meat is thoroughly defrosted, it's time to get the trimmings ready. Make sure you do this a few hours before you intend to cook. Top and tail the mixed peppers, clean out the seeds and rinse well. Slice the peppers into long strips, then square segments. Peppers are very tasty but also add bright colour to the kebabs. It's all in the presentation. Prepare the onions in the same way (but don't rinse them!). I always use red onions as they hold their flavour and texture better in the

searing heat of a barbecue. Rinse and halve the cherry tomatoes, then simply quarter the mushrooms. They need to be on the large side so that they hold to the kebab skewers. Too small and they'll fall off during cooking. Take another long swig at the Stella Artois. It's a chef's prerogative.

Rinse the cubed rabbit meat and pigeon breasts and pat dry in a kitchen towel before you start loading up the kebab skewers (I use steel skewers; they are re-usable and help heat the meat from the interior). Load them up in any order you like. Use your imagination but make sure there's a good mix of meats, colour and flavour to make them attractive to your diners. I always load up a few skewers with pure meat – no vegetables or sauce – just for Dylan and any visiting dogs. Dogs loves barbecued rabbit or pigeon and it's a damn sight better for them than the sausages your guests will sometimes sneak their way.

By the way, that Stella Artois should be getting low by now. If it isn't, you're not enjoying the experience enough.

Once the kebabs are made up, spread them out in a shallow tray and brush them generously with the smokey BBQ marinade sauce. Make sure you're preparing these early enough to place the tray in a fridge for a couple of hours to let the flavour seep into the meat. If the Stella's finished, crack the first bottle of Sangria.

Cooking and Serving

Braise the kebabs slowly at the top of the barbeque, turning the skewers regularly. It's hot work but the Sangria will help cool you down. Test the meat portions regularly with a sharp knife to ensure they're cooked right through. Balance this against over-cooking the vegetables.

To serve, scoop the contents of the skewers into a serving dish with a fork and invite your guests to eat them in whichever way they choose. I love them wrapped in a warm tortilla bread, covered with lashings of mayonnaise and relish. Delicious. Others will eat them as a side-dish or sweep them into a baguette.

Wash your kebabs down with the second bottle of Sangria and enjoy the plaudits your guests will lavish on you for producing such an uncommon and yet tasty meal. If they didn't like it, you'll be past caring anyway. Sangria has that effect on you. By now you're probably describing in full detail how you bagged each rabbit and pigeon they've just eaten. That will sort out the shooters from the non-shooting types and pretty soon you'll be left with the guests whose company you most enjoy!

By the way, I had a vegetarian version of this recipe but I've forgotten which bits you leave off the skewers.

August

Gold–Dust

Golden ears and stalks fall 'neath the blade
And billowing dust erupts at each sweep made.
Deep within the standing crop, there's fear
Whiskers twitch, as noise assails the ear.
The Hunter stands nearby with loaded gun
To intercept each bolting rabbit's run.
Some will run the gauntlet, some will wait
But, one by one, the Hunter seals their fate.

Autumn magic

It was one of those days that will stay embedded in my memory forever. As I closed the last field gate behind me, I sensed an omen. A sparrowhawk watched me from its sentry-post on a telegraph pole. As if conceding its terrain to a fellow hunter it swooped down, circled around above me and flashed out across the top of the stand of ripe cobs. I drove the Jeep under the cover of the woods which overhang the huge maize field. The warm, blue August sky was pebble-dashed with grey and white cumuli making threats they would never deliver.

I dropped some hide-nets from the edge of the beech canopy and set up a corvid 'egg-raid' scene on the ride nearby. Then I hid away to await anything 'incoming'. It was a long but pleasant wait. Crickets drummed in the long grass and crane-flies danced to their beat. A green woodpecker flew down to join the dance, hopping about trying to catch the little long-legged helicopters. My crow and magpie decoys just perched nonchalantly, guarding the rubber eggs, clearly unimpressed with the comedy enacted before their unblinking eyes.

Wildlife drops in

A carrion crow was duped first. It fluttered down silently onto a post, head bobbing and turning as its coal-black eyes surveyed the scene below. Decision time. A ground shot would be easier than an elevated one but I sensed it wasn't convinced by my

A simple decoy nest scene

fake cameo. A bird on the cusp of flying will open and close its wings, feinting an approach. This crow just watched – until a pellet tucked neatly into its neck, finishing its vigil. I returned to mine, still waiting for my true target to arrive. A flock of goldfinches entertained me for a while, skitting along the tops of the maize spikes.

Unexpectedly, a large dog fox broke from some secret hole in the rabbit netting lining the side of the field. It pondered the scene from a distance, sensed danger and crept into the maize looking every bit the villain. I pulled the camera from my bag and a 'squeaker' from my gilet pocket then tried to lure the fox back into view. You don't shoot foxes with air-rifles (even at FAC power). These large predators need much more power for a humane dispatch so I restrict my attentions to photographing them. This wary visitor was having none of it, though. I could see the maize stalks waving as he crept up and down a few yards into cover. Inquisitive, but wise.

To my surprise, my calls were answered by the harsh chatter of a pair of magpies. These were my intended targets but I had not expected them to respond to this. Each time I squeaked they returned with a chatter, in unison, yet they were deep under the cover of blackthorn bushes. They moved nearer with each exchange, sensing an easy supper, no doubt. I kept squealing, gun at the ready, and with a flash of black and white one leapt onto the post which had graced the crow earlier. It met the same fate, but with much more elegance,

and its partner fled with a shriek.

I broke cover to retrieve the two corvid corpses then settled down behind the nets again to watch two nuthatches and a robin engaged in some sort of territorial dispute. The robin won, a feisty little cock looking all the 'guardsman' in his scarlet waistcoat. A roebuck ghosted from the maize some distance away and browsed on the ride for a while. It was an hour before the second magpie returned and found the lure of the eggs too much. An unhealthy decision, as it turned out, and it joined its cousins in the ditch.

Pause for the sunset
I cleared the nets and decoys into the Jeep to go walkabout as the sun dropped. Stalking a rabbit along the field's edge I was puzzled at the strange set of ears that

It was an unhealthy decision to visit my eggs

popped up in my scope. I set down the gun slowly and eased out the camera. Kneeling up, I caught the fallow hind staring at me over the rabbit's head. As she stood, the rabbit fled, but there would time for rabbits later.

Edging on, I then disturbed a muntjac leading a tiny fawn. It's a rare day that I see all three local deer species in one field. Progress was slow, scanning for the tell-tale translucent ear tips of my quarry. More than once I was startled as green woodpeckers screeched from ground to tree. These emerald birds are becoming common and they are as much a nuisance to the stalker as the vociferous jay. Their alarm call registers for half a mile, warning all cautious creatures that man is on the prowl.

Around the margin I crept and chanced twice on grey squirrels raiding the maize

The fallow seen across the rabbit's head

kernels. Both fell to the gun and at last, I also got my rabbit for the pot. I had sat for a while in the half-light listening to the hooting of a tawny owl urging the moon to rise. The rabbit hopped out to graze just 25 yards away and posed perfectly in the rifle scope. Having dressed her out I sat again quietly, watching noctule bats pouncing on midges mid-flight. Their dark shapes fluttered, moth-like, against a sky diffused with the pink and lilac hues of the dying sun.

Night falls

Before the last tendrils of light were withdrawn beyond the distant tree-line I was treated to that wonderful spectacle, the rook procession. Legions of dark wraiths passed over my head, migrating from the feeding fields to some distant, hidden roost. Their companions, the jackdaws, wheeled and rolled among them, like sheepdogs herding a flock to some distant pen. Soon, the harsh cries of corvids were replaced with the melancholy sound of the tawny owl. As one hunter finished, another was about to begin. In the gloom, the rearguard woodpigeons clattered in to roost nearby.

Driving out of the farm I texted the farmer, Olly, as promised, to let him know I was finished. The mobile rang back. 'How'd you get on?' he enquired, so I told him. 'You know what?' I commented. 'Your farm is a wonderful place to be at dusk'.

'I know,' he replied, 'It's magic, isn't

it?' As he rang off, the little owl that had been watching me from the fence post in my headlights went gliding off in front of the Jeep. This small raptor is my favourite bird and one which I associate with myself as a hunter (I named my canoe *Little Owl*). Small, wide of eye, vigilant, lonesome and seldom seen. Magic indeed!

Spring power, straight shooting

I don't keep many rifles in my armoury. There really is little point. A reliable legal-limit PCP for general hunting, an FAC powered PCP for specialist hunting trips, a small CO2 powered Ratcatcher whose name accurately describes its purpose (a useful farmyard indoor gun, low powered and for short range shooting) and a couple of legal-limit spring-powered rifles. One is a break-barrel, the other an under-lever system.

Like most shooters, I cut my teeth on break-barrel spring guns. The lightweight .177 calibre Diana I obtained surreptitiously forty years ago, at the age of 13, started a desire to hunt that would never leave me. Popping starlings (allowed back then) at ridiculous ranges for such a feeble gun, using open sights (scopes were something soldiers and secret-agents used) set me on the path to becoming proficient with a gun. Learning how to handle recoil; how to relax into a shot, how to

sight up accurately, how to judge range and therefore hold-over or under, how to breathe correctly, how to follow-through on the shot – all this is valuable schooling. Learn how to shoot a modern, full power spring gun accurately and you've jumped the second hurdle in becoming a proficient hunter (the first being knowing your quarry intimately). When you progress to the more expensive (more maintenance demanding) pre-charged pneumatic (PCP), you will find shooting accurately a breeze.

Pre-charged Pneumatics v Springers
So why would a man with a couple of PCPs in the gun cabinet keep his springers? There are many good reasons, the main one being education, but let's examine a few.

Pre-charged pneumatics, as their name suggests, require a charge of air from a pump or a diver's bottle. When the air's used up, the shooting finishes until you can re-charge. For walk-about hunting, it's highly impractical to carry a supply with you. With some models (like my Weihrauch HW100K) the air reservoir is removable and small enough to carry a spare. Not too much of a problem. With a spring-piston gun, you have no such burden. As long as you have ammunition, you can shoot. So if I'm planning a long day (or night) in the field, a springer is useful.

Weather is a factor, too. PCPs rely on a discharge of air from that reservoir at a given pressure. On extremely hot or

Regular practice with a springer keeps the eye keen

cold days, that pressure level may vary and affect the gun's accuracy. No such problem with spring powered ammunition. The PCP has a delicate air-seal technology. Damp and rain can call for higher maintenance, particularly if the weapon has been drenched. The springers are less demanding and very robust, so an ideal choice when I'm planning to be out in inclement weather. There are downsides too. They are noisier on discharge than a PCP, even with a moderator in place, though that noise is relative to the distance from your quarry. What sounds like a crack at your muzzle is a mere snap 30 yards upwind. No, by far the biggest disadvantage of the spring gun is that single tiny pellet loaded in the breech and the time it takes to re-load another pellet.

I can re-load a break-barrel faster than an under-lever. Usually in about 4 seconds if I've got the next pellet in my palm ready. But that 4 seconds is halved when cocking a multi-shot PCP, where the scope doesn't even have to leave your eye during the process, the cocking bolt or lever doing what you have to do with your fingers and hands and eyes on a spring gun.

I mentioned 'education' as an advantage. For all the reasons stated before. I find that when shooting with a PCP for months on end I can become complacent. The crucial 'follow through' on a shot becomes slack, therefore missed shots become more frequent.

The absence of recoil allows a firmer grip on the stock, itself a shooter's sin. Consequently, trigger technique deteriorates and I tend to snatch instead of 'tickle' the trigger. When I sense this, I go back to a springer for a few sessions. On targets, paper or metal, the spring gun will exaggerate these faults and I can correct them. To hit a one inch circle on a paper target at 30 yards with my springers requires a controlled and relaxed shooting discipline. It requires good trigger technique and breathing control. When these are fully perfected on targets, I transfer the training to live quarry.

Today, after just such an exile from the PCP, I'm testing myself back in the field with the under-lever, a Weihrauch HW97K. The static target exercises are over and I'm confident enough to tackle vermin. Confident enough, even, to venture after that lively little target, the grey squirrel. That means I'm also happy with my re-loading technique which is the hardest to recover after a 'time-out' on a single shot gun.

Greys are notorious for taking a shot but running on, and many a shooter has laid down his gun because he can't handle the 'karma' of injuring but not dispatching a squirrel. Should a second shot be needed, you need to be quick. The PCP is ideal for this but the proficient spring gun hunter can achieve this too.

I load a pellet and hold a second one in the palm of the hand supporting the fore-stock. This serves two purposes. It ensures I keep a relaxed grip on the stock and that a pellet will be easily available for a fast re-load. I didn't need to use that second pellet today, taking out two squirrels and a rabbit. But some days I do, I must confess.

On the subject of injury of quarry: don't be fazed by it. It happens, and it's far better that a hunter accepts the fact (and prepares for it) than stays in denial. There is more on this subject in another chapter.

The springer is the 'desert island' gun: low maintenance and no air bottle is needed

Kits and karma

I can think of few pleasures in life that give me the satisfaction I enjoy sitting under the cover of a hedge and ambushing rabbits on a warm evening. A lowering sun screamed at me to draw an air rifle from the gun cabinet and take some solitude in the fields after a busy 'family' weekend. I have wonderful and tolerant kin around me but I'm a man who can easily feel crowded. So, not even my faithful lurcher tonight: he had already enjoyed a lengthy trot in the low temperature of a hazy dawn.

This evening I sauntered to a choice spot where a grassy border meets a wood and I sat, contemplating, under a parasol of lush beech boughs. I bathed in the soft rays

Proficiency with a springer guarantees results with a PCP

of the setting sun which cast long shadows on the maize stalks laid out before me. Crop-laden woodpigeon flashed along their flightline and the rooks began their slow, laboured journey to who knows where this fine evening. The distinguished call of a green woodpecker rang across

out a pair of translucent ear-tips making semaphore signals above the greenery. Then another pair.

By now my scope was at eye-level and the safety catch was off. One pair of ears edged forward and a brown, whiskered face appeared. It was so passive, so calming here

Twilight – a magical time to hunt

the thicket and the hypnotic murmur of collared doves lent a tranquil air to the surroundings. Deep in the nettles, which were half grown and desperate for rain, I sensed motion. My shooter's eye picked

that I was loath to disturb the karma. The hunting gene kicked in, however, and the coney dropped quietly among the nettles.

I settled back as a worried woodpigeon clattered from the thicket beyond and a throng of previously invisible rabbit kits scuttled beneath the fence and sank from sight into their nurseries. I reflected that if I was to walk the field margins now, there would be rabbits in abundance and ripe for shooting. On such a beautiful evening, with an itch scratched and a fat rabbit for the pot, why not just content myself with that? The swallows were hawking midges low over the furrows, my tanned face was glowing and all was right in the world. So I decided I'd just sit back against a tree and watch the twilight unfold. It would soon be time for the pipistrelle bats to change shifts with the swallows so the gnats would get no rest. The fallow herd (swollen to over forty beasts and in need of thinning) would be abroad, no doubt. Who knows, maybe the barn owl would bless this watcher with its ghostly sweep across the meadows? There is good Karma in this place tonight.

The following day saw me melting in sweltering heat, behind a leaf-net hide. Not pigeon-shooting but resuming the perpetual struggle against the coneys that are picking off the tender barley shoots before they can rise. I was about set to withdraw, satisfied with my efforts. Quenching my thirst with a chilled bottle of white wine on my garden deck and scribbling some notes had a huge appeal as a prospect.

But behind me, in the copse, a rustling delayed my exit. A small muntjac deer, seemingly unaware of my scent, crept out into the field and foraged some way before seeming agitated. It rushed back into cover, behind me, and browsed to within yards my hide, still oblivious to human presence. I had exchanged the rifle for the camera. A white scut caught my eye beyond the deer. I was torn by the desire to photograph the muntjac and to shoot the rabbit. But the muntjac won the day, or maybe it was the rabbit? My farmer would have cursed the triumph of art over ordnance. With the right artillery, he'd have had me shoot both.

If the glut of rabbits I've culled so far this year is indicative of the situation nationally, there must be hot rifle barrels, weary lurchers and knackered ferrets all

A muntjac at touching distance

over the country. It's hard to imagine a Britain without this non-native animal. In just 900 years it has become the country sportsman or woman's staple quarry and is responsible for supporting an entire eco-system including fox, badger, buzzard, stoat, weasel and polecat. Perhaps even the odd big-cat? It also feeds the corvids, thanks to that recent invader of the countryside, the motor vehicle. Every night the lanes and highways are strewn with small tyre-crushed victims and at dawn magpies or crows are busy cleaning up.

Warrens have materialised along previously sterile hedgerows and today I watch kits far out in the drillings while the sun sits high. The adults are much more judicious, of course, and have learned the danger of such exposure. That's why they've reached maturity in a species in which 75% will expire before a year old. Yet these same kits will reach breeding age within four moon phases and today, as they frolic in the sunshine, I wonder if I've been too lax this season?

Some of my farmers ask why I don't employ the shotgun. My answer is simple. For every ten I could hunt with the scatter gun, two would drop and eight would take flight, deafened. With my PCP air rifle I'm likely to hit eight, accurately and selectively, while two may escape.

I thought I'd be patient this year and cull them when they were large enough for the pot. Big mistake. Lord, don't let farmers 'Google' any aerial photos of their land before harvest, for they would see the damage I have allowed to occur through that decision!

Rabbit shooting is called-for

During the past few weeks, my desire to 'cultivate' the warrens has evaporated completely. The fecundity of these pests has stunned me. There are even more than last year (and that wasn't an idle one). It would be criminal of me to put the growers, who graciously let me on their land, out of mind. That permission is for a purpose: to protect crops. Thus, much as the culling of young rabbits often feels wasteful, I am obliged to prune the kits heavily now. I've shot over thirty (and many adults, too) on three farms in the last two days. This took around five hours of shooting, not a bad score with an air rifle in broad daylight. Imagine what the gun-lamp would bring? For I suspect this plague may well demand an early start to lamping. Myxomatosis is almost inescapable, with the warrens so packed, but will

Rabbit damage to a sugar-beet crop

come too late for arable farmers. I shot many rabbits last winter that were pocked survivors of this awful blight.

In six weeks or so (when these kits are plumped up) there will be the largest meat harvest available that we've seen for half a generation. Now wouldn't it be sensible if the hunter, the country butcher, the urban supermarket, the British household and the 'credit crunch' all came together to put rabbit back on the national supper table? It would also be the excuse for many aspiring young shooters to persuade their parents that they need to buy an air rifle. Alas, in the age of fast food and the ready-meal, it won't happen.

Routine maintenance

My air rifles take a bit of a kicking in the field. They're busy guns and are taken out in all weather. It's not just the shooting action that adds wear and tear to steel and stock. They go through barbed wire and over gates. They get bumped and knocked. I lean them against trees and they fall over. They are laid on damp grass or dirt, get pushed through brambles and holly and occasionally get dropped accidentally.

On one occasion I was straddling a barbed wire fence in a wood when I was tripped by some hidden wire beneath the leaf mulch. I ended up with my crotch snagged on the top wire, legs either side, before tipping over. My sub-12 ft/lb

A harvest there to be gleaned

HW100K was thrown about ten feet as I released it to break my fall. I wasn't the slightest bit concerned at the arse being ripped out of my camo trousers. Nor the six inch gash on my inner thigh. It was seeing the rifle bounce off the woodland floor that brought tears to my eyes. Once I'd checked that the wedding tackle was integral, I ran straight to my rifle to check it over. It was totally unblemished. After a few test shots, it hadn't even lost its zero.

Between hunting sessions, I take care of the old girls and they're really not very demanding. Of course, they carry a few war wounds (particularly on the stocks) which all tell a tale. Modern PCPs are pretty robustly made and a little bit of regular servicing keeps them functioning sweetly. Usually, that means after about every 500 shots. Though they get some extra attention if they've been out in the rain or snow. So, how do you keep a PCP air rifle in shape?

Well, firstly it goes without saying that

141

you must make sure the rifle is unloaded and the breech clear before performing any kind of maintenance. The magazine should have been removed before you left the field anyway. So now, with the magazine out, cock and fire the rifle outdoors, into a soft surface such as the lawn, to be certain the barrel is clear.

Next, you need to undress the gun a bit first. Remove the silencer (assuming you have one fitted). Unclip the sling if you use one.

Now separate the action from the stock. On most PCPs this is simple, just a couple of Allen screws, so takes only a minute to do. This is particularly important after a drenching, for reasons I'll expand on later. Don't fear doing this; it won't affect your zero. The gun's zero is relative to the barrel and the scope so it won't be interfered with. You are now going to clean the stock and action separately.

Cleaning your gun

First, the action. To clean the inside of the barrel thoroughly, cut a piece of coated garden wire (or fishing line) about three times the length of the barrel. Double it over and slide the looped end down the barrel from muzzle to breech. Pull out the loop from the breech fractionally (about half an inch). Now cut a piece of thin cleaning rag to about two inches square. Roll it into a tight swab and spray it liberally with a solvent gun cleaner.

Next, tuck the swab into the loop you pulled out from the breech. Now draw the wire or line slowly back through the barrel, from breech to muzzle, until the swab pops out of the muzzle end. It will be covered in the lead deposits that are lining the barrel and choking the power, so repeat this two or three times with fresh swabs until they come out clean.

Many shooters neglect to do this and some claim that the build up of lead deposits improves the gun. This may be true if they are using pellets which don't fit tightly into the breech. They would be wiser to find a wider pellet. All I can say is that on my guns, power can improve by 0.5 ft/lb if I do this regularly. For that reason, remember to fine-tune the gun's zero when re-assembled.

Now put the silencer back on. Personally, I wrap my silencers in camo duck tape. This protects the casing and ensures that when it's poking out of a hide, nets or bush, it's less noticeable to vermin.

Coat a felt pad or rag <u>lightly</u> with gun-oil and work it gently over the steel while the action is off the stock. Oiling the hardware drives off any moisture and fingerprints. It prevents rust on the blueing; and while the stock is off you can get to all those parts normally hidden from view, such as around the trigger guard and along the bottom of the air cylinder. Be careful not to get excess oil around the trigger sears or any air ports. All you're doing here is light maintenance.

Now it's time to oil the software too (the stock). This helps to cover up those war wounds and protect the woodwork from rain, dew, snow and blood. Yes, blood is acidic and will mark both stock and steel. I use gun-oil for general lubrication but if I'm attending a deep scratch or dent, I'll use a bespoke stock-oil.

I mentioned earlier about the importance of separating stock from action after a drenching. This allows both the benefit of a good air-drying before oiling as described above. Moisture sitting in pools inside the stock can cause severe rusting on the action, particularly on the underside of the air cylinder. A rusted air cylinder is an accident waiting to happen, for obvious reasons. Having dried and oiled both sections, put them back together.

Finally, clean scope. I always use a lens-pen for this job, easily found in good camera stores. Remove any scope covers or sunshades. Use the fine brush at one end to take away all the dust and debris that accumulates when you're out and about in the woods and fields.

Next, use the cleaning pad on the other end to work gently from the centre of each lens outwards in circles until the

Look after your gun and she'll look after you

lens is glistening. Clean, crisp optics mean rapid and accurate target acquisition.

Finally, put a few drops of oil on the sling swivels to keep them quiet then fit the sling back to the gun. Just like your car or your house, a bit of regular maintenance saves lots of grief and expense later.

Cleaning the scope with a lens-pen, easily found in good camera stores.

Foxburgers

Don't worry: the name is just a bit tongue-in-cheek. I got to thinking what Reynard would ask for if he went into MacDonalds. It would be rabbit-burger, of course. The following sumptuous recipe produces thick quarter-pounders that can be served up as an evening meal or char-grilled on a summer barbeque. The kids love them. You'll need a mincer and one of those little burger-making devices found in many kitchen shops. My electric mincer and the idiot-proof burger moulding kit came from Lakelands in Norwich for less than £50. Rabbit meat is very lean, like chicken, so doesn't lend itself too well to burgers unless mixed with a more fatty meat. You can use minced pork belly or sausagemeat. Either will add a sticky texture and let you pat out the perfect burger.

Hard to imagine these were once hopping around a Norfolk field

Ingredients

to make 6 quarter-pounders
3 rabbits (saddles & hindquarters)
½ lb of sausagemeat
¼ lb of bacon
1 large onion
Salt and pepper

Preparation

Bone all the prime meat from the rabbit saddles and hind legs. Cut the rind from the bacon and have the sausagemeat close to hand. Feed all this through the mincer, using a coarse filter. Make sure you mix it up, feeding rabbit, bacon and sausage meat a handful at a time each. Then, finely dice the onion and mix it into the meat thoroughly. At the same time, season with salt and pepper. You should end up with a bowl of 'doughy' meat paste.

Place a wax paper into the base of the burger mould and spoon the paste into the mould, smoothing it firmly. Keep filling until the top of the mould is level and you've pressed out all the air bubbles. Put another wax paper over the top and push the completed burger out onto a plate. Repeat this until the meat is gone. Place the burgers in a fridge until you're ready to cook.

Cooking and Serving

If it's a winter night indoors, grill the burgers steadily on a medium setting for about 12 minutes, turning regularly. If it's a summer barbeque, keep them at the top of the griddle and turn even more

An electric mincer is worth its weight in gold

frequently. Don't let the outside blacken. With both methods, run a knife through the middle to check they're fully cooked before serving.

For an indoor dish, serve with roast potato wedges, black pudding, fried mushrooms and peas. If it's a barbecue dish, serve with fresh chopped salad, lashings of mayonnaise and new potatoes dripping with butter. Don't worry about the calories or the cholesterol. The rabbits were vegetarians... and look what happened to them!

Burger kits like this are cheap and easily available

September

Fall

The swirling autumn mist that cloaks the dawn
Battles with the sun to win the morn.
The lurcher works the hedgerow with its nose
And marks the spot wherein the quarry rose.
The Hunter stays the dog and takes the trail
Through dew-damp stubble, out towards the bale.
Amongst the shredded stalks he spots his beast;
The whisper of his gun assures a feast.

Gold and grey

Driving home from work along country lanes on a late August afternoon a haze of yellow dust billowing like a sandstorm above the hedgerows catches my eye. Those dinosaurs of open agriculture, the combines, are at work scything down the golden barley. With their floodlights and modern GPS tracking systems they'll be working through the night to bring in the crop before the next deluge in this abnormally wet summer. I pulled over to watch the monster gobbling up stalk and grain, its driver a mere dot in middle of the eye of the leviathan. I drove away to prepare my kit for the morning, eagerly anticipating the end-product of the barley harvest on this farm: Adnams ale.

Stubble shooting during harvest
I always strike while the iron is hot when the barley comes down. The woodpigeons and crows would be on the stubble early tomorrow to mop up the spilt ears and I wanted to be there before them. That night, before I drew down a pint of that ale, I gathered together my nets and decoys. The gun was checked and filled with air, magazines loaded and the alarm clock set for sunrise. I sat on my garden deck that evening with that beer in my hand watching a crimson sunset: a hunter's delight. So I celebrated with another pint. And (I confess) another. Before I took to my bed, I checked the digital barometer in my study and was pleased to see the weather was indeed set fair for the morning.

The sharp edge of the desire to hunt can be easily dulled through over-indulgence, so when the clamour of the alarm clock failed to rouse me, my good wife did, with a nudge to remind me that she had just been woken up for a reason. Bless her. As I dressed and collected my kit, Dylan was following me around the house whining. It was his plea to accompany me, but he would be disappointed today. That same whining would have no place in the patient vigil behind a hide net, in searing heat, that I intended. With a feeling of guilt but (from experience) good intention, I left him behind.

Burying the Jeep under cover in the wood, I set up my nets close to the field's edge but under the cover of the green canopy. Even at this un-godly hour I disturbed magpies and crows, nature's earliest risers. I checked the breeze before setting out a small squadron of flock pigeon decoy shells, randomly but mostly facing the current, between 30 yards and 40 yards from the woods edge. I set a crow decoy beyond one end of the pattern and a magpie decoy some distance from the other end. Finally, I set a Pathfinder target at 30 yards along the wood's edge, in sight of the nets.

There was grain aplenty on the floor. I settled behind the nets on a tripod seat. I use one of those revolving affairs – to wait for incomers. I lined up the Pathfinder in the scope and took a shot, missing. A second. A miss! Both just high and right. Off came the turret caps, a few clicks on both elevation and windage turrets. Shot three and took the centre out of the small target. Gun zeroed. Back to the wait.

Waiting and watching

The wait, for me, is part of the enjoyment. This, for me, a man to whom inactivity and idleness comes hard, is forced relaxation. It's watching time. The camera will be close by. The fox hurdling the un-baled lines of straw, the wild cock pheasant strutting out with its harem, the distant hare jinking across the stubble (a rarity on this farm), the grey heron floating toward the river margins for its breakfast of frogs, the family of weasels frolicking along the grass ride.

Many folk sit and watch this on TV, mouths agape, unaware that it is all happening at the end of the field at the edge of their town, everywhere, every day.

The woodpigeon is a prolific bird and its control is really the realm of the shotgunner. It is caught much more easily in flight than on the ground. Yet the challenge for the airgunner is no less enjoyable. Picking off birds that land (momentarily, mind you) to inspect the decoys is an art that needs practice, not least because even a stubble stalk can deflect an air rifle pellet.

The woodpigeon is masterful in flight and a joy to watch

The feeding bird is rarely still and you need to be opportunistic. Many birds will land among the pattern but few will present a stable target. Some will look about momentarily at the fakes and fly off, suspicious. Others will settle in comfortably and start to feed. These are the target birds, so a good deal of patience is required. Once you take the shot, hit or miss, the others will fly and the waiting starts all over again. If I'm honest, half a dozen to an air-rifle shooter is a red letter day. Some days I'll get more; but mainly less. The taste and versatility of the pigeon breast makes it all worth while, though the primary reason for being here is crop protection.

As stated above, the enjoyment is not just about the shooting. Watching hundreds of woodies casting about the fields is an awesome sight. Circling, swooping, veering away, free-falling, they are masterful aviators and so fast, too. Watch their antics when the sparrow-hawk appears. The pigeon will jink like a rabbit with a gazehound on its tail, they will brake and plunge like a peregrine and they will accelerate, to flee, like a missile. The hawk will work hard for its supper and often go hungry.

Shot birds among the decoys need attention from time to time but I try not break cover too often. I'll set them up as extra deeks, removing any feathers blowing around (they will warn incomers of danger). Those that come back into the hide are bagged. On a wet day, I will cut out their breast in the field, before I leave. Today is fine though, so I'll pare out those juicy fillets under a running tap, to contain the downy feathers. Crops will be examined before disposal. They will reveal

Woodpigeon on the stubbles

the bird's diet and give me clues as to where it fed, for I make a point of noting the local farm crops as I drive about. This, in turn, will advise where to check for flight lines and set further patterns.

The morning draws toward noon and the high sun beats down at my hide. Not only am I slowly melting but I'm also getting what I describe as 'net-fever'. Each time I look out at the army of decoys, swelled by shot birds, I start to lose perspective. Range finding becomes more difficult. I have to keep counting the decoys. Is that one an incomer, or one already shot? I swear that dead one is moving, but it's the stir of breeze on feather.

There is a natural lull anyway. Pigeons tend to feed and roost, to digest, then fly out to feed again. I'm not going to wait for the second flights; I'll go crazy. So I venture out to collect my decoys and fold my nets. It's been a fair outing. Though seven birds will have the shotgunners cackling into their ale and the farmer raising his eyebrow, the breasts will simmer deliciously in a casserole this winter. A few whole birds, wrapped and packed in the outdoor freezer, will add to future patterns and there will be seven less birds plundering the winter barley seeds as they are sown in just a few weeks time.

Of Gods and gunners

As the autumn harvest nears, you'll find me driving around watching the crops with all the anticipation of an expectant father, just like the farmers. I want to be able to judge when the crops are going to come down and I'll plague the farmers with phone calls to get them to call me before they do. Why? Because for the shooter, there is a short-lived window of opportunity which I never want to miss. The barley cut.

Dawn patrol

This weekend started with a dawn patrol around the dew-sodden fields. Travelling light – just lurcher, game-bag and rifle – the wet boots were sacrificed. A silver sun struggled to burn off the morning mist as this hunting team, man and dog, steadily picked off several rabbits stealing their way twixt the standing barley and the hedge after their night's raiding. They hop out from between the golden stalks to pause on the greensward before heading into the briar patch, that impenetrable fortress where I can't reach them. Dylan collected the fallen while I hocked and hung along the way to save any burden.

The lurcher was in his element, nosing up partridge and pheasant along the way, forbidden game, for both him and me on these fields, whatever the season. He stood trembling, eager to chase, when a roe pricket stepped from the barley fifty yards from us. It was a Mexican stand-off but a simple, whispered *'leave!'* stayed the dog. The deer bolted along the margin and I thought how tempting that white rump must look to a hunting dog. His training has been so valuable, particularly around stock, and that simple command has saved many an embarrassing situation.

My eye was drawn to the barley-ears ebbing and flowing like a golden tide in the morning sunlight. I picked a husk and chewed into the grain, which was firm.

A woodpigeon's crop guides you to where the flock is feeding

sweep. Billowing yellow dust followed the leviathan and it was tracked by the trailers that follow alongside to collect the grain. The crop here is destined for processing into Robinson's Barley Water, that old Wimbledon favourite.

The woodpigeon were already massing

Plundering the drillings

The cut must be close.

The weather forecast for the coming week was heavy rain and it wasn't hard to reason that today looked ideal for the combines to sweep in. A quick mobile phone call to the farmer confirmed this. My plans changed immediately. I set about collecting and paunching my rabbits, then headed home to gather some different kit. Not good news for Dylan – but he'd had an enjoyable outing in the coolest part of what was to be a glorious day. This wasn't going to be a day for carrying heavy gear so I loaded the Jeep with light decoying gear, a dozen woodpigeon shells and a camo leaf-blind. As I would use the adjoining copse for cover, I didn't even take hide-poles. The nets could be hung from the foliage.

When I got back to the field, the combine harvester had already made its first

in the hedgerows and the copse to pick off any excess grain spillage from this process. I set a decoy pattern close to the wood's edge and as the combine harvester passed by I gave the driver a wave of acknowledgement. He must have been amused to see me here again, as he does every year.

The modest breeze was kind to me today, crossing in front of the copse from left to right. I set the shells in a standard horseshoe pattern, leaving the front of the shoe open to allow wary birds an escape route. Pigeon will look for this before daring to land. The prongs of the horse-shoe (the two rear decoys) acted as range-finders, with the furthest from the tree-line paced at 40 yards, the nearest at 20 yards. Any bird that dropped within those two markers would be within easy range for the air rifle.

By now it was high-morning and the sun was beating down on the open field. I settled into the cool shadows of the wood, covered my exposed skin with insect repellent and covered my upper body with a lightweight camo top and cap. The midges were already swarming around me.

As I watched from the wood, the combine's huge concentric cuts gradually reduced the island of standing barley in the centre. Several rabbits and a hare (rare on these fields) bolted from the receding crop and dashed for the wood. Before long, the decoy pattern attracted the attention of the pigeons wheeling around above the harvester. A few came in to settle. Scoping up the bobbing grey heads of woodpigeon amongst the stubble is a challenging process for the airgunner and his single, small pellet. A barley stalk can easily deflect a pellet.

Slowly, steadily, throughout the morning I notched up a decent tally and occasionally left cover to add shot pigeons to the decoy pattern, pegging them with snipped coat-hanger wire I'd brought with me. An over-inquisitive crow lingered far too long and paid the price, joining the other dead birds in the pattern. I also

A dawn patrol in the autumn mist

bagged a couple of pigeons that dropped onto nearby branches to study the decoys. Effective as the insect repellent was, I had still managed to pick up more bites than pigeons so far.

The lumbering machine continued to level the barley field until a stand of barley about 100 yards square remained. The operator stopped and I watched as a 4x4 appeared. I'd seen this acted out before so I ventured out to collect my decoys and the remaining uncollected birds.

I stowed my kit and stood at the wood's edge to watch the cull. The driver of the Range Rover stepped out, pulling a shotgun from its tailgate. He broke the gun, loaded it and waved to the operator of the combine harvester, who set about the final cut. The shot-gunner strode up and down as the machinery flailed and I saw him snap the gun shut several times and bring down bolting rabbits with the admirable skill of an experienced rough-shooter. He enjoyed his sport and some meat for his table. There were no fox, deer or hare in this last stand, although there often are, and I headed away to breast out my pigeons.

Breasting pigeon

I always do this under the cold tap in the kitchen sink so that the wet feathers don't scatter. It had been an enjoyable day, thanks to some prior planning, though I had an uncomfortable

night, even dabbing witch-hazel on those midge bites. Next morning I re-visited the stubbles at dawn. That forecast rain was still a couple of days away and I knew that the long hurdles of barley straw would have to be baled before the rain spoiled them. I left, promising myself that I'd return tomorrow to check.

On Monday morning I drove up to greet a rustic scene which never fails to impress. Huge rolls of baled barley straw thrown randomly across the stubble as though the Gods had thrown a party the night before and left their discarded champagne corks on the lawn.

The lurcher and I sat in the shade of one of these bales, close to a copse, to pick off a rabbit and a brace of rats who ventured out to scavenge fallen grain among the stubble stalks. A squirrel did the same and met with a pellet, to join the other fallen quarry.

The Gods had left their champagne corks in the garden

The rats were cast into the nettles at the edge of the pit, where their own brethren would no doubt cannibalise them. I kept the rabbit and squirrel, though. I had a use for them. Both corpses were laid on top of nearby bales as bait for passing corvids.

Dylan followed me into the shade of the copse, relieved to be out of the sun, and we lay waiting for something to spot the bait. A few rooks made curious passes at the bait but were reluctant to land and soared back up to float on the thermals. Even the magpies weren't around today; it was too hot for flight. I was beaten, eventually, not by impatience but by the clouds of mosquitos who abandoned the festering pond deep in the copse at the scent of blood. My blood! I cleared away the bait after its long exposure in the heat, throwing it into the copse for Reynard, and headed home for a long, cold and well-deserved lager.

It had been an idyllic weekend for an air rifle hunter – but it could so easily have been missed without some prior intelligence and a good relationship with the farmers.

Stealing souls

For some years, long before I took to scribbling pieces for shooting magazines, I carried a camera in my game-bag to record some of the wonderful things any shooter sees when out and about with a gun. You only need to look at my humble pictures, particularly the early ones, to realise that I

I always have a camera nearby

am not a professional photographer. Mostly I snatch what I see, to record a moment in time forever.

The native Australian Aborigines, when they first saw images of themselves, were distraught at the photographs and thought that their souls had been stolen from them.

Today, many celebrities would probably think the same, stalked by paparazzi. The Aborigines were right, you know. The captured image rarely lies. Sure, modern digital photography allows the expert to be creative, perhaps deceitful, but it also allows the natural history photographer to crop and enhance images and to store a library of moments that most people can only ever hope to enjoy on TV.

The invitation into photo-journalism for the shooting press forced me to think carefully about picture structure and content. Helped along with good advice from editors, particularly Nigel Allen, former editor of *Airgunner*, the pictures got better. To this day, though, I use a simple digital camera and I'm still reluctant to get dragged into the arena of the professional wildlife photographer. The SLR camera is far too complex for my hunting field. Most of the photos you see in this book are taken with a Fuji Finepix S8000fd. It looks like a mini SLR and has a 12x optical zoom which is ideal for wildlife pics. The 8 megapixel resolution gives enough quality for magazine reproduction.

The other camera I always have with me is another Fuji. the Finepix E900. This is a pocket-sized compact with 9 megapixel resolution. It's always tucked into a pocket in my camo combat trousers for easy access and those random, opportunist snaps. It also has a great macro function allowing me to photograph close-ups of plants, animal tracks or trails or other sign.

Often, I'm as happy to walk away from a hunting trip with a set of quality images as I am a sackful of rabbits. Hide shooting, for instance, can involve long periods of inactivity. The camera adds another dimension and I've stolen the souls of many birds and animals who have passed by my hidden position over the years. Some of my favourites are shown within these pages but there are hundreds of others archived on my PC and on hard discs.

Using a bale as cover

Harvest time: a short-lived opportunity

Working as a photo-journalist

Magazine photography can be amusing. Many readers assume that when they see a picture of me recovering a dead squirrel or preparing for a shot, that I have a professional photographer following me around all the time. Indeed, some magazines actually do this and send a house-photographer out with the writer/shooter. Most don't. Nor would I allow it. Hunting is difficult enough without a media entourage. The text I write is true and accurate – I wouldn't do it otherwise – but some of the pictures are re-staged using a self-timer. The wildlife and quarry photos are real-

time pictures. Over the past few years I've been asked by several readers who took the pics? I have a stock response. 'My lurcher, Dylan, is highly trained but this was the most challenging task I've ever taught him'. I've never had an answer back!

Creative photography is as challenging as rough shooting and looking for opportunities for a photo now comes naturally, such as sunset shots or a dawn mist. These can add atmosphere to what would be just another dull picture of a guy with a gun.

I see nothing wrong with adding a selective photo to an article either. For instance, a crow at its nest when I'm writing about crow shooting, although the nest might be 'illustrative' rather than the actual nest I've been targeting. This is simple practicality. If I spent time snapping close-up pictures of a crow I'm about to shoot, it's unlikely to hang around long enough to allow a shot! Rabbits are different. I'll often snap them from a distance if I need fresh library pictures. Then shoot them with the gun.

Awkward photo moments

Talking of library pictures, I've had some hilarious and embarrassing moments trying to get photographs. Recently I stopped in a lay-by on a busy trunk road near me to snap a pair of crows tending their nest. The male abandoned his task of feeding his mate at the sight of the Jeep beneath the nesting tree. The female sat tight on her eggs and all I could see was her beak. A bit of ingenuity was called for. I have several recorded bird sounds on my mobile phone which I use as ringtones. As I wanted to get some shots of her in a protective stance, I played a recording of a sparrowhawk 'chiming'. It worked and the threat made the crow jump onto the side of her nest looking for danger.

So there I was, standing by the side of the road with a camera clicking in one hand and waving a mobile phone in the other. Unfortunately, absorbed in this task, I didn't notice one of Norfolk's finest pull up in his squad car behind my Jeep. The first I knew of it was the crow's flight and the slam of a car door. I turned to see a traffic cop strolling toward me with his hands on his hips.

'Is there a problem, sir?' he quizzed. My explanation was met with a frown when he looked up at the nest. 'What crow?' he asked. I explained that he'd just frightened her off. 'So why were you waving your mobile phone around?' I was impressed with his power of observation and mumbled a lie about trying to record the crow's calls. He gave me a stern lecture about distracting other drivers and asked me to move on. As he left, he threw a look over his shoulder which clearly said 'Nutcase!'.

Then there was the time I was photographing a tribe of about fourteen winter magpies in a public park in Yarmouth, where I work. As I was snapping away, an elderly lady passed by, walking her rug-rat. I wanted a picture of the group in flight and they'd spotted the dog, so I kept filming as she passed. She stomped toward me waving her stick and asked 'Why are you taking pictures of me? Are you some sort of pervert?' I looked at her and the expression 'bulldog chewing a wasp' came to mind. 'No, Madam, I was photographing the magpies'. She looked around her. 'What magpies?' Of course , they were long gone. I was tempted to tell her they'd been frightened off by a shrew, but thought better of it.

On another occasion while driving to work, I stopped to take some photos of shot crows pegged out on little crucifixes in a farmers field. A fairly common sight in Norfolk but not nationally, so I thought the use of these bird scarers would interest magazine readers. As I was snapping, a Range Rover screeched to a halt behind my Jeep. The farmer, clearly irate, jumped out and blustered toward me. 'What you

One of Dylan's pictures: not bad for a dog!

doing, chappie?' he demanded. 'Who gave you permission to photograph my land? You some sort of bloody *anti?*' I sighed deeply and thought to myself that sometimes the rural community really does make a rod for its own back. I explained who I was and what I was doing. I pointed to the BASC stickers on the Jeep. As I was dressed in the work uniform - suit and tie - he was confused but suddenly more receptive. I gave him one of my 'free vermin control' business cards. The subsequent piece in *Shooting Times* commented on how there were no rooks in his field, but the adjoining crop of mustard seedlings were being plundered. I hope he read it. It was a compliment to his initiative.

Photographs of dead quarry often become an emotive subject. There is a faction within the shooting fraternity that objects to the printing of such images, stating that they serve to fuel the 'anti-shooting' activists.

Personally, I don't think that stopping such pictures would make an iota of differ-

Some of the best photo opportunities occur when you wish you had the gun in your hands

ence. If people are biased and narrow-minded, they will find fuel anywhere. If the shooting press placed a self-imposed embargo on pictures of dead quarry, the 'antis' would not only claim a moral victory but would also assume that shooters feel guilt at culling quarry.

The important thing for the shooting fraternity is to maintain the status quo, to respect the opinions of others but to resist attempts to force those opinions upon us. For the photo-journalist, the dead quarry picture is a no-win situation anyway. I've run quite a few articles where I've deliberately excluded quarry pictures, only to be accused by readers of embellishment, because there was no photographic evidence!

C'est la vie.

A hare on the field margin – a shot for the camera, not the air rifle

The squirrel squad

I watch the TV screen in dejection as the commentator lauds the dexterity and reasoning skills of a grey squirrel raiding a bird feeder. The theme tune to *Mission Impossible* accompanies the footage as the producer does his utmost to mystify what is simply the instinct of vermin. Intelligent and opportunistic these aliens to the British countryside may well be but I can't help wondering if the commentator would be so approving watching a burglar in his house on his CCTV? Because in nature's terms, that's what I'm looking at here. This sort of anthropomorphism simply augments the public's ignorance of the ecological destruction wrought by this little pest.

How I wish they'd started the documentary in the eight acre spinney I

was given permission to 'manage' a few years ago. Not an isolated copse but the small corner of a 100 acre spread. I'm not allowed into the rest of the wood, which is owned by someone else, and therein lay the problem. The diverse species of trees – ash, beech, oak, pine, hazel, birch and more – should have been resonating with birdsong. But for almost every tree, there was a scruffy drey and the copse was over-run with grey squirrels.

It has also been more than two generations since our native red squirrel had ventured here and it will never appear here again in my lifetime. It was driven out of its habitat by the ferocious territorialism and pox-ridden presence of *Sciurus Carolinensis*. It didn't stand a chance. When I took this small corner of Norfolk under my wing, though, there was no way I could abide

woodland devoid of birdsong. So the grey squirrel pogrom began from day one.

Culling Grey Squirrels

In the first exploratory winter in the copse, the squirrel execution squad accounted for about 60 greys. This was enough to encourage some of our hardier native bird species to risk nesting there again. The return of blackbird, thrush, robin, blackcap and chaffinch was our reward. But during the nesting season, the tree-rat team kept up its unrelenting attrition. With the vast, neighbouring forbidden forest bordering this small plot, I felt like King Canute trying to hold back the waves. Nature, as we know, abhors a vacuum. The grey squirrels just kept coming and still do, to this day, though they don't survive for long.

An intimate knowledge of the copse allows me to plan our forays so that we can hit the enemy on their runs and highways. Because what that TV commentator failed to relate is that the grey squirrel is a creature of predictable habit and exceptional greed, both of which make it susceptible to the hunter. Ironic, is it not, that the TV presenter (a leading light in the RSPB) calls his squirrel 'Sammy' and feeds it with peanuts while I (a shooting man) cull it ruthlessly to protect our indigenous songbirds? Nothing should surprise me, though. On BBC's *Springwatch* one year, they persuaded a farmer to adopt a family of orphan jays (Jimmy, Jane, Jasmine and Jeremy?) I nearly choked on my whiskey. Sorry, I digress.

So, what constitutes this 'squirrel squad', you may beg to ask? Simple, it's yours truly, my .22 calibre HW100K and my lurcher, Dylan. From time to time, we bring in a fourth member, my lad, Sam. And a highly effective team it is, too, accounting for over 200 grey squirrels in this small copse alone over the three years. Not to mention many hundreds more on other permissions.

Though fieldcraft, experience and accuracy with the rifle makes me a key member, the team would be less effective without the dog. Dylan's vision, audible range and sense of smell have combined to double the numbers we've hit. The more mature he gets, the wiser he gets and his understanding of this form of hunting tempts me to speculate that he prefers it to rabbit stalking. Today we were in action

Public enemy number one

The squirrel pogrom began on day one

without Sam. A second man on a squirrel team gives good advantage but the lurcher has quickly learnt to imitate that task. I will explain later.

Approaching the copse quietly, I slipped through the gate with Dylan close at heel. The leaf mulch on the woodland floor was moist after overnight rain and muffled the fall of foot and paw. We were out early, just an hour after sunrise, knowing that the greys would be most active in another hour.

Squirrel courtship opportunities

Early September is a time when this year's young males are chasing the females for the opportunity of 30 seconds of union. Their courting is frenetic and, when the pursuit is on, the squirrels are careless of threat – fairly typical of the male of any species, I think we'd admit. This is where Dylan comes into his element. We were set up close to a fence separating my permitted copse from the 'forbidden forest'. I was clothed in camo, but more from habit than need. Huddled close to a beech trunk, I'd laid the dog beside me and already his ears were scanning like those huge satellite dishes at Jodrell Bank, picking up noise far beyond my audible range. His damp nose was twitching, his eyes sparkling.

He sat up, ears pricked forward, his eyes focusing into the distance. He was trembling with anticipation. Occasionally, he threw me a frustrated glance which said *'C'mon! Can't you see it?'* I couldn't, yet! Then, a light grey apparition scrambled across the leafy floor and hopped up onto a fallen tree trunk.

I whispered to the dog to 'stay' and gently lifted the rifle to my shoulder and measured the huddled form through my scope. 40 yards. A bit far but heading this way. It scuttled off the end of the trunk, ran to a mossy bank and sat up on top. 32 yards. The murmur of the pellet leaving the silenced rifle was innocuous as the squirrel flipped. The dog, still quivering, looked to me and I gave the fetch command. He dropped the retrieved corpse close to me.

We settled down again. This time, Dylan sat up like an alert stoat when he sensed another approach. There were two of them, a male following a female, running. They were too fast for a shot. They scurried up a beech, chasing around the trunk, only 25 yards away. I needed to halt them, so I whistled. One sat up on a bough, hissing at me. The other was pinned flat against the trunk. I chose the sitter, just as it moved and I missed. Damn! It leapt up and off across the canopy. The other scurried around the trunk, out of sight. I send in the dog and he knew what

Spotting and retrieving – Dylan's team role

threat but revealing itself to me. With the squirrel spread-eagled against the tree, it was an easy shot. Dylan almost caught it as it hit the floor and he brought it to me with an approving wag of his tail.

Two down, and it was still early. It was looking to be a good day for songbird protection. As if on cue, the sharp 'Tack, tack, tack' of the blackcap reminded me we were invading his space. Cheeky little bugger! Someone ought tell him who holds the mortgage on his freedom!

Dylan drives a squirrel around the trunk

A good man and dog team can cull hundreds of greys

to do. This is what my 'second man' Sam, would usually do. A squirrel reacts to movement and will hide from it. It would seem that the star of *Mission Impossible* has no memory and can't count.

Dylan circled the trunk widely and slowly, approaching from the opposite side to me. The squirrel edged around the trunk, keeping blindside of the moving

October

After Dark

As eyes adjust to dark, the Hunter quakes
The lurcher at his side now sits and shakes.
Primeval... man and dog and blackest night,
Together they will hunt. Their weapon... light.
The dog stands up, his fur and ears erect,
The Hunter flicks a switch and eyes reflect.
Flick off, judge range, flick on the lamp once more
Now shoot, flick off and back to darkness raw.
The Hunter sits the dog and settles heart.
How many stayed? How many did depart?
The light back on, a sweep, reflections new,
A waggled beam to stop the fleeing few.
Select just one, in range, line up and fire
Did it drop... or did it make it to the wire?
The Hunter looks to dog, just lying there
He knows... that dog... the hunting field is bare.
The Hunter sends the dog across blind land
For cold, wet nose will seek, retrieve to hand.
The Hunter stands, the dog heels in on cue
It's time to move and hunt a pasture new.

Bunnies in the beam

If it wasn't for that fecund agricultural nuisance, the rabbit, I would have very little permission on which to hunt and even less excuse to carry a gun or run a lurcher. The British country sportsman owes much to this largomorph, the staple quarry of many a shooter, ferreter and falconer. I will make no attempt here to relate the history of its presence, a subject much recorded by better and more eloquent scribes than me.

My love/hate relationship with the coney, however, can't go without mention. It has the capability to make me feel guilty when I fail to control it sufficiently, yet to cause dismay and frustration when its absence denies me a full game-bag. Usually, the rabbit's behaviour is as predictable as the lunar cycle. Yet sometimes it can confound and confuse even the most experienced hunter. A passive animal, it has at times brought to me feelings of guilt, remorse and compassion. Yet it has physically hurt me, unknowingly, both directly and indirectly. While its presence has gained me land on which to shoot, it has also caused loss of permission. I have hunted it with snare, ferret and dog over the years but no method has been as enjoyable – and please note I didn't say as efficient – as hunting it with an air rifle.

Tonight I intend to make reparation for those idle summer evenings when a leisurely stroll with gun and dog were curtailed in favour of watching the late sunset from the comfort of my garden deck.

With a rabbit or two in the bag (and the knowledge that dusk would bring better results) I must confess that a cool glass of white wine, a small cigar and a scribble in my notebook were far more appealing. I keep seeing a platitude adorning the rear windscreens of many Land Rovers around here. It reads '*One Life: Live It!*' and who am I to argue? This is the man who used to adopt the 'Carpe Diem' philosophy (Seize The Day). Funny how that attitude changes with age.

So now, with October's fierce winds, the deck canopy is drawn in and the furniture stowed mid-ships until next spring. The planters and pots have shrivelled. The bird table is still visited but by drab, native regulars. The white wine has been replaced with smooth reds or warm whisky. The clocks will soon be changed and dusk is now but a whisker beyond the end of the working day. At this time of year I spend more time studying moon-phases than daylight conditions, keeping

an eye on hunting opportunities and the right conditions for lamping: low winds, a hidden moon, little rain. Tonight is such a night. A lamping night.

Instincts of the gundog

As I gather together the kit I will need, Dylan is wittering and whining in true lurcher style, skulking far too close to my boot. On a normal day, the rattle of the keys to the gun cabinet (half a house away) has him pacing and squealing like a stuck pig. To watch me test the lamp's beam against a wall has him bouncing off the ceiling, for he knows he will be going out with Master, something never guaranteed in daylight. If the hide-nets come out, he will watch me with a question in his doleful, brown eyes. His pleading will bear no fruit as the impatience of a lurcher, squeaking annoyingly behind cover, is no recipe for successful ambushing.

Tonight, however, his presence will be invaluable and he knows it. I think he senses something else too. My dislike of lamping contrasts with his affinity for it. He is my crutch and at five years old, he plays to that role as an old hack does to a novice foxhunter.

So, the kit? Travelling light (excuse the pun) is the order of the night. A small game-bag, but contained within is a large bass-bag. A net bag capable of holding at least six or eight rabbits. A sharp knife. The mobile phone, that plague of modern technology for the working man, but good insurance out in the dark. A cap light, spare torch, pellets, rifle, camera and a squeaker (in case I want to photograph foxes). The gun-lamp is a bit special tonight. It's a new LED type which snaps on top of the scope and is controlled by a pressure switch on the stock. With about 7 hours continuous burn-time and a 70-yard beam, this little compact light source means I won't be tripping over cables. Those old-fashioned lamps running off a battery in my pocket or bag were so frustrating. I had to detach the umbilical cord every time I crossed a gate or fence. This has a filter kit, too. I'm using amber this evening as I've lamped here before. Next time, it will be a red filter, though I use red reluctantly. It kills the beam too much. As I'm shooting my silent legal-limit Weihrauch 100K tonight, I want only as much distance as the rifle's range, and the amber filter will tone it down a touch.

Bumping the Jeep down the track toward the target meadow, I switch down to side-lights for the final approach. The

Dylan's senses will be invaluable after dark

purr of the diesel engine will have alerted the coneys, so I rig up the gun under the low light of the tail-gate. Dylan lies in the back, head in his paws, watching every move.

Dressed for the cold

The frosting of his breath reminds me to pull a pair of shooting mitts from a bag. I'm dressed for the cold but not too heavily. My hat and snood will keep the heat in, and once we get moving, my body temperature will rise. My sturdy walking boots are water-proof – the dew will lay heavy tonight. I slip the bag over my shoulder and sling the rifle over the other, loaded and ready but with the safety catch on – always, the safety catch on – so important in daylight but doubly so in the

An amber filter tones down the beam

dark. The slip goes around Dylan's neck and as he jumps down, I shut the tail-gate quietly and lock the Jeep. The flash of the orange lights annoys me slightly but that's why I've parked so far from where I intend to hunt.

As we slip quietly through the metal gate to the meadow I congratulate myself on fore-thought. I've been around all these gates during the past few weeks with a tin of WD40 to lubricate the catches.

Dylan's demeanour, whiskers twitching and ears alert in the facing breeze, alerts me to close quarry. It's too soon. We settle close to the gate and I squat next to the sitting dog. His right paw is up, stroking the cold night air, marking.

Night vision

We will wait, though, to let the meadow settle and to allow my eyes to adjust to the gloom. After a few minutes, I can see the contrast between distant tree-line and sky. Even in this blackness, I can see about 15 yards out into the field. We move on, towards the warrens along the hedgerow. Following the hedge, we move slowly and stealthily until Dylan tugs slightly at the lead and looks toward me. I kneel and tap his rear quarters. He sits.

I bring the gun to my shoulder, one eye in the scope and the other open too. I push the pressure switch and a swathe of orange light cuts through the black-ness. Three amber discs reflect back at us, within range but close to cover. Light off. The rabbit's eyes are on the side of its head. Three reflections mean three targets but I don't want these ones. I move the dog behind me and he obeys, reluctantly. I aim the gun out into the field, 45 degrees from the hedge, and push the switch. Six, maybe seven, eyes flash back at me, varying ranges. Lamp off. A couple were within 30 yards, I think.

Range-finding to a light is difficult and your perception changes with the colour of the filter. Our eye is used to seeing the full form of a rabbit and our brain is programmed to judge its distance. When it sees only the eye, there is a tendency to think that it is further than it really is. That makes us over-shoot. Before I turn

Hocking and hanging allows you to work unburdened

the lamp back on, I remember this.

As the cone of light sweeps out again, I pick up a rabbit at 35 yards, adjust to 30 and shoot. As it flips, I release the switch, trying to mentally picture where it fell. Lamp on again quickly. One runs, I waggle the lamp and it squats, confused. Number two goes down, but as it does, two or three others leap out of the grass and bolt. Quickly, I turn the barrel back to the hedge and wave the light, then kill the beam. They won't all cross that beam. Light on, slightly out into the field. Two squatters, the first too close, the other at 25 yards. I shoot and miss. That will have been 20 yards then! Now, a quandary.

Retrieve or not to retrieve?

Do I retrieve the rabbits or move on? I sit in the dark for five minutes then flick on the beam and sweep the field, behind me, back toward the gate. I pick up two sets of moon-like discs. In one corner, there are two eyes set close together and low to the ground. In the other, two wide-set eyes but higher up. The former, a fox. The latter, a deer, though I'm not sure of the species. Quandary over. The rabbits need to come home to the bag. I'm not in a mood to let Charlie steal my kills. I've even had a fox run down the beam of my lamp like a lurcher to snatch a coney just as I was about to shoot it! That's one of the thrills of an evening's lamping: you just never know what you'll experience!

This is where the lurcher earns his place in the team again. Without the nose of a dog, finding and recovering shot rabbits in the dark can be a trial. I try to memorise the landscape where each kill drops (a tussock, a stand of nettles, a fence-post) to make recovery easier. Scouring around for ages with a torch will spook every living

Paunching out in the dark – this should keep Old Charlie away from the hen house

creature around. There are still many rabbits out in this meadow, further on. I don't want to disturb them, and the quiet air rifle wouldn't have spooked them yet.

We walk out in total darkness and I whisper to Dylan to 'look about!' His nose leads me to each shot rabbit. The subtle cap-light, a small LED fixed to the peak of my baseball cap, allows me to collect the shot quarry and we return to the hedge. Using this low beam, I hock the rabbits

and hang them high out of Charlie's reach. Now we can move on up the lea, unburdened, and continue.

Man, dog, lamp, gun

The evening continued like this. Working the meadows, man and dog, gun and lamp. Hauling shot rabbits back to the Jeep is hard work, made easier by paunching them in the field. As we approached the first three, still hanging in the blackthorn bush, I turned on the lamp. Two orbs blinked at me then fled. They say the fox is a cunning creature but he's just a thief and an opportunist. Flashing the beam back to where I had just gutted some other rabbits, there was already a fox feasting on the free supper. We stopped to gut these coney's and I threw the innards into the open meadow. The frustrated vixen would get her feast tonight, and better this than my farmer's hens.

Decoy days

Decoys tend to be associated most with pigeon shooting and wildfowling. The image that immediately springs to mind is a pattern of fake grey pigeon shells, or perhaps dead woodpigeon, laid out over a crop; or perhaps fake ducks or geese bobbing on wetland pools.

The word 'decoy' was derived from the Dutch word *'Eendekooi'*, meaning 'duck cage' which dates back to the old practice

Some of my decoy collection

of luring ducks onto water and funnelling them into a wicker cage.

Strangely, decoying is mainly confined to avian species. Though predatory mammals sometimes show an interest in decoys (I've had both fox and squirrel visit mine) they aren't as easily fooled. There is a growing trend in using battery operated 'critters' (which shake and squeak) to lure foxes and I hear they're quite effective on corvids too. I use several types of decoy fairly regularly. Let me take you through a few examples from my collection and how I apply them.

Falcon decoys

The peregrine falcon is one the largest and most imposing of my decoys. Set out in full view, menacingly guarding a dead rabbit, it will drive any of the crow species wild. Scouting rooks will soar in to circle the intruder and call their alarm, bringing dozens more into to mob the 'deek'. Most birds will stay airborne but some will perch in nearby trees to scold the peregrine. Hidden nearby, under a hide or nets, I target these perchers. Shooting one from a bough will double the fury of the mob.

If it goes quiet, I add any dead corvids to the scene around the falcon and withdraw the rabbit. The reaction to this 'victim and murderer' scene when the birds return can

172

be unbelievable – reminiscent of a Hitchcock movie! This avian chaos invariably draws in inquisitive carrion crows and magpies too.

Owl decoys

Carrion crows and magpies are notoriously difficult to get close enough to shoot with an air rifle. Place an owl decoy near a nesting pair, however, and they will instinctively stay close to the nest to protect it. Both species will mob and attack the threatening decoy if there are eggs or chicks in their nest. With no nest to protect, they usually try to avoid the decoy though. A well-covered hide, set close to the nest, will reap its reward. I use both a little owl and a large, gaudy

My little owl decoy – effective on nesting corvids

American great owl in equal measure. The larger decoy is so easily seen, it is ideal for woodland. The little owl decoy is perfect for the field margin or the farmyard. Because it is so small, the little owl decoy is one that's often in the game-bag waiting for its opportunity.

Crow decoys

I generally use two types of crow decoy: a full-bodied, flock-coated bird and a foam 'flyer'. Used together, they make for an effective scene and the advantage of flock or foam (rather than plastic) is that they don't shine in sunlight or rain. That tell-tale glint can be enough to chase off your quarry. I usually set up the full-bodied decoy out in a field, with the 'flyer' hung in a bush. This set-up draws distant, passing birds towards the scene. Shooting will be from deep cover or from a hide. Depending on terrain, it will involve shooting either perchers in the trees or ground shots. For the latter, a gutted rabbit placed at a reasonable distance from the decoys will tempt crows to feed. They will always land out of range, 60 or 70 yards out, then hop in cautiously toward the bait, so patience and absolute stillness is needed. I ensure that I'm within range of the rabbit, but not necessarily the decoys.

Watch out for magpies coming in too. They can't resist an easy meal but their greed often leads to their demise. The magpie will flash straight down to the bait. If my crow decoys are out but I'm not getting visitors, I use a crow call. It only

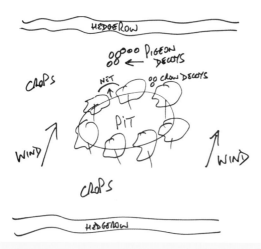

It pays to have a plan when decoying

takes one curious crow in the vicinity to make for a successful stake-out.

Magpie decoys

My pair of flock-coated magpie decoys probably get more use than any of the others. Magpies are fiercely territorial throughout spring and summer. They will react aggressively to any intruder of the same species. It's this principle which makes the Larsen Trap and its use of a live Judas bird, such a success. The magpie will

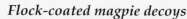

Flock-coated magpie decoys

*Setting a pigeon shell pattern
on the stubble*

usually confront an intruder with beak-to-beak combat, so you're looking to shoot around the decoy itself.

If I ever needed convincing that my flock-coated decoys were more realistic than my old plastic ones it came when I watched an ardent first-year male magpie trying to mount one of my flock decoys, staked out on a dung pile. It was such a hilarious moment, it saved the youngster's life. I couldn't possibly have shot it, I was laughing too much. It knocked over the decoy in its excitement and flew off, indignantly!

Pigeon decoys

Like most shooters, I have a selection of pigeon decoys tucked away. Lightweight plastic shells, flocked shells, full bodies, flyers and a dozen Silosocks decoys. These little flat-pack pigeon-shaped windsocks are terrific for the air rifle shooter. You can easily stow a dozen in the game bag and place them when you spot a flightline. The breeze fills the ultra-violet-coated socks making them billow and bob, looking like a feeding flock.

If I'm on a serious woodpigeon mission, I take everything: shells, fliers, full bodied and Silosocks. You can never set out enough. The air rifle hunter is looking for static birds to shoot (on the ground or on the branch) so the decoy pattern isn't as crucial as for the shot-gunner. The need to study flight-lines and pay attention to wind direction and range is just as important, though. The addition of a flock-coated crow decoy near the pattern will add a sense of security for any curious woodies. They know that the carrion crow is not a bird that wantonly puts itself in danger.

Decoy eggs

I used to use real hens eggs to bait in crows or magpies, breaking them to expose the rich, yellow yolk. On a visit to a local toy store with my lad, some rubber eggs caught my eye. They looked so realistic, I bought three. With some artistic use of a scalpel and fabric paints, I created a permanent broken egg from one, with the yolk exposed. Set out next to a magpie decoy or in a home-made nest set on the ground, they look the real deal. They have brought in crows, magpies, jays, even squirrels, for a closer look. The nest scene is never elaborate, just open enough to attract the eye of passing vermin. These decoy eggs are now a permanent feature in my kit bag.

Free meat, no takers

Modern times and modern consumerism have spoiled the nation's palate. I confess to finding it amazing that the folk who shop weekly for the insipid processed meat on their supermarket shelf turn up their noses in disgust when offered wild rabbit. Year after year we are surrounded with one of Britain's most healthy, abundant

You can afford to experiment with free meat

and free harvests. On the weekend drive to the supermarket these same people will pass (obliviously) a wealth of free meat as it browses in the hedgerow and field border. The shopper will scour the butchery shelves and buy (in their thousands) water-filled poultry, factory-processed red meat, not to mention sausages and burgers whose constitution leaves much to be desired. They will look out (and waste good money on) chicken and fish products such as fingers, escalopes or pies stuffed with the detritus that a respectable fox would decline. Offer them a few pounds of dressed, jointed wild rabbit portions and they will walk away quickly, making all kinds of excuses. Yet what you have just offered them is free of charge, free of additives, free of fat and free of controversy – the ultimate organic meat. Fed, unwillingly, on the very best the farmer can grow. No battery farm, no captivity, no chemicals, no genetic tampering, but to the average Brit, 'No thankyou!' Why?

The main reason is that the British consumer has long since forgotten how to prepare wild food, so it intimidates them. Despite the best efforts of several celebrity chefs, the average Brit just doesn't want to get their hands messy. They would rather either buy second-rate, pre-prepared meat or pay for top-grade, butchered meat. Don't get me wrong, I'm not knocking the local butcher and we have a superb one close to me. He is barely surviving due to competition from the big three supermarkets (equally close to home). His

Prime, lean meat fed with the best the farmer can grow

field yesterday.' (Before their lights went out, these animals enjoyed fresh food, lots of exercise and even a healthy sex life. Can you say the same for that chicken in your fridge?)

Rabbit meat is certainly not a 'staple' in my household, despite my easy access to it. I've had to get adventurous with it to encourage it to the family table. Some of my recipes are in this book. These days, once on the plate, it's always a welcome meal. The family favourite has to be rabbit and sausage casserole. Marinaded for hours and slow-cooked in a tomato sauce with mushrooms, onion, leek and peppers, served up on a bed of mashed potato, Yorkshire pud and peas – it's a delightful winter Sunday dinner.

prices reflect that attempt at survival. The overheads he bears can't compete with the big players and their bulk-buy, economy-of-scale negotiating powers. But will he buy my shot rabbits? No – because most of his customers just won't eat rabbit!

I hear all sorts of excuses when I offer rabbit to friends, family and work colleagues. *'Haven't got time to prepare it'* (I've done it for them: skinned, boned, washed, cubed and ready to cook). Or *'Myxomatosis'* (Sorry, but I never bring home myxied rabbits). Then *'Tapeworm'* (I know that the rabbit is clean, I skinned it myself: did you ask the same of that supermarket pork?). Perhaps the worst excuse being *'You shot it? How cruel!'* (Sorry, but shooters don't act cruelly. Clean dispatch is the order of the day). *'I can't bear the thought of eating something that was running around a*

Now and again, we do have rabbit pie but it will be filled also with leek and pigeon breast. We also use rabbit for summer barbeques, skewered with peppers, onion and mushrooms, dripping with a variety of BBQ dressings. Coneyburgers are also a favourite on the barbeque and they're fun to prepare. Prime rabbit meat from the saddle and haunch are run through the mincer with sausage meat and a few pigeon breasts to add colour. Then packed with different flavours so that the eating is a culinary lottery. Chopped apple in some, leek in another, chilli powder, grated cheese. You can afford to experiment like this when the meat is free.

Sometimes I wish this was the office

Remember Mrs Beaton? She did have a point when she reputedly said, *'first catch your rabbit'*. Suffice to say, clean meat will attract more takers. The rimfire and airgun headshot rabbit will offer untainted meat. So will those caught with snare and ferrets. I know many who won't eat shotgunned quarry, due to the random pellets. Free meat is one thing, a hefty dental bill another!

The advantage of having a mincer at home, though, is that even meat which you wouldn't want on your table can be processed for the dogs, ferrets or hawks. My lurcher often enjoys a cooked, minced coney mixed with some biscuit. Not too often though: it's a treat. I wouldn't want him crunching into those plump rabbits he retrieves!

Balancing work and shooting

For those of us quietly obsessed with hunting, the need to get out from between four walls to walk the woods and fields is an addiction. I'm sure I'm not the only hunter who often spends some part of my day at work looking longingly out of the window, desperate to escape! I'm a management professional and so my career in public service means hours cooped up in office buildings, often attending long meetings.

Years ago, I considered a life-change and thought about re-training in an agricultural or forestry role. I'm also a family man and (sad but true) the prospect of a rural salary would have meant much sacrifice for my family. So I have ploughed on, keeping my family *'in the manner to which they are accustomed'.*

To be fair on them, that is really no sacrifice, as I get little complaint about my constant excursions with gun and camera! So, it's all about that old chestnut: work/life balance. Compared to many, I'd say I'm lucky. It didn't take my own boss long to realise that if I punctuate intense periods of high productivity and success with short bursts of relaxation with the gun and the dog, he would benefit too. So he's quite flexible about time off and if you're an employer, you would do well to consider this.

Reaction of work colleagues

The stark contrast between my business suits and my camouflage shooting gear would astound many of my work peers, few of whom have ever seen me in magazine articles. Nor would they, for they don't share the same interests as me. It was amusing in a recent enviro-crime forum when a slide popped up showing me in full shooting gear pointing a rifle.

Now, as you can imagine, a forum like this consists of a social spectrum which includes everyone that the term 'equality and diversity' can cover. The presenter quipped 'and if enforcement fails, there's always Ian!' The looks around the table said it all. Several people looked to me, then the picture, then back again. Some smiled, but a few looked quite disturbed by the image, including some senior local government officers. None of them dared to voice the negative comments they may have been thinking, for they know that I tend to defend through attack and can be quite eloquent when I do so. Lips were sealed but, judging by expressions, opinions were formed.

Though I have no reason to hide my activities, some people have an issue with hunting and the culling of vermin, so I don't actively promote my alter-ego in the professional arena. Prejudice could be a career-killer. The 'gung-ho' image, with no other context to explain it, could have played into the wrong hands. Thankfully, no harm was done.

On the opposite side of the spectrum,

as a senior manager responsible for over 200 front line staff, the reaction from most 'blue collar' employees is totally different. I run a portfolio of public services in a Local Authority: refuse and recycling collections, grounds maintenance, building maintenance, street cleansing etc. These are 'salt of the earth' folk who spend every day clearing up waste and fly-tips, repairing vandalism, pruning, planting, grass-cutting and generally trying to improve the environment of their neighbours. They get more brickbats than bouquets because, in the public's eye, they don't do it fast enough.

When I arrived a few years ago, I was quick to voice my opinion (publicly) that they are social heroes. They don't litter, spew and defecate on the street. Some residents and their children do. They don't vandalise parks, playground equipment, cemeteries, buildings. They don't pull up shrubs and floral displays. Some residents do. These guys (and girls) just come in, clean up and repair the damage.

If you're wondering where I'm going with this, you will be interested to know that 20% of my staff unwind from this constant pressure and undeserved criticism through involvement in country-related activities: shotgun, air rifle, rimfire, centre-fire, ferreting, part-time keeping, beating,

Is this the image of a senior manager in public service?

photography and voluntary conservation work. A walk around the yard when the work teams are setting out or coming back in is always a pleasure.

Many of them know what I do, outside work, and they often want to talk about it. They buy the shooting periodicals. There's a lively exchange market amongst themselves, trading all year round: pheasants, partridge, rabbit, venison, woodpigeon (even salmon, though don't ask from where!) There are more Firearms Certificate holders in the organisation than senior managers. I work hard on employee relations to ensure that there is no revolution and call-to-arms!

Vermin control in the workplace

In almost any workplace, there is the opportunity to meet people who may need a little help with vermin control. Feral pigeons from buildings, rat problems in the warehouse, even the nuisance rabbits at the end of the garden. There are also situations you have to reluctantly let go. Our depot (in the midst of an urban setting) attracts magpies, crows and gulls who come in numbers to scavenge on the back of the dustcarts. We have a fox family living in the scrub at the back of the yard. Though many of the workers would have murderous designs on these species, there is another group who view their presence as entertaining. So they're left alone.

There is one colleague who fervently disapproves of the shooting of vermin. Our views on this are totally polarised, yet we spend many moments discussing bird or mammal sightings, sharing knowledge and even comparing photographs. He recognises my love for wildlife but finds my willingness to cull certain species totally at odds with that concept. We agree to differ but the relationship, the sharing of experiences, gives respect on both sides.

Family life and shooting

Perhaps the most important side of work/life balance for the recreational shooter relates to family. While kith and kin may tolerate your absence while you bring in the money, many will find long absences in the field with a gun less acceptable. Again, I confess to being lucky. My gorgeous wife understands me well enough to know (like my boss) that periods of solitude with the gun or a camera clear my mind and bring me back relaxed and more attentive. If I'm showing signs of stress, she pushes me out with the gun and the lurcher. She knows it's far better for me than a bottle of pills or a trip to the pub. In turn, I make sure I don't over-do the privilege.

Family events take precedence over shooting (although I have been caught photographing magpies at a wedding instead of the family groups!). It works for us.

There's an old adage: *'All work and no play makes Jack a dull boy'*. Like many of these old sayings, it evolved for good reason.

November

Silhouettes

Through glove and cap and coat the chill pervades
As winter's fragile sunlight slowly fades.
The Hunters wait — the lonely woodland hour
Draws to a close as eyes, the dark limbs scour.
As flash and crash of quarry fills the wood
The flock comes home to roost, the light still good.
The Hunter marks each settling, huddled form,
He fills the bag and heads for home and warm.

Roost shooting

October's swirling gales have swept the last of autumn's mosaic from the crowns of the trees. The dark sulking boughs of oak, ash and sycamore spread like arms across a gun-metal grey sky, as if in surrender to the onslaught of winter. Trudging through the sodden grass I note the shoots of winter barley struggling to break through the sopping clay that is their bed. In the midst of this vast field, a ring of trees that surrounds the old marl-pit looms through the drizzle like a ghost-ship emerging from a cold sea-fog. I brace myself before crossing to the pit, knowing that the viscous mud will cling to my boots and every step will become harder, more treacherous, than the former. No matter. This toil will be rewarded, for the pit is a very extraordinary and mysterious place.

This hollow is a desert island amidst a wide, flat ocean of arable ploughland. The straight mile to any line of trees in the vicinity is broken only by low hedge-rows, making the pit a point of respite and sanctuary for any transient creature daring to make the journey from horizon to horizon.

A cautious circuit of the pit on a fairer day can reveal (as it has to me, often) the prints and paths of its many visitors. Indeed, I have surprised most at one time or other and I've observed all manner of bird and beast take flight at my approach: fox, fallow, roe, squirrel, hare and a host of birds including barn owl, sparrow-hawk and heron. There is a humble rabbit warren here, neighbour to a wider rat colony. The small, festering pond in one corner is a watering post for wild visitors though at the height of summer there is low water cloaked with a million midges. Lord knows the level of leptospires in this natural trough?

The pit's ancestry is an enigma. Squatting in its gloom, one can imagine orcs and hobgoblins delving for some dark purpose yet the trees tell the truth of its age. The acorns and sycamore seeds probably took root in my fathers youth – and I'm no sapling.

Shooting with a silencer

On this murky November afternoon, however, I wasn't too concerned about the quadrupeds that visit this sanctuary. The pit is an expedient stop-over point for flocks of woodpigeons and an evening roost to hundreds. The trees lining its banks are smothered with ivy and mistletoe, giving dry security to the nocturnal squatters. There were no nets or contraptions this afternoon, just my most vital tool.

My whisper-quiet pre-charged pneumatic air rifle is designed for such a domain. The silencer emits little noise at the muzzle and, being a carbine, the gun is easy to work with between bough and sprig. The rotary magazine and sleek side-lever cocking mechanism allows for rapid re-loading. The 50mm scope mounted on top would maximize light gathering in such poor conditions yet still I choose to fit a sunshade to my optic. This stops the gleam from the lens spooking my quarry, enables swift target acquisition and prevents drizzle or moisture from clouding my view.

Shooting woodies as they wing in to roost is a simple process if you've practised elevated shots. At the edge of the hollow, I kicked the clods of mud from my boots, set down my bag and laid the gun against a tree trunk. I checked the breeze and affirmed I was on the lee-side of the pit. Pigeon will always opt for the least breezy side of a roost, for obvious reasons. I had already disturbed several birds with my approach. Inevitable, but they'd be back.

Dressed from head to toe in dark camouflage clothing (though dull browns and greens will suffice) I also wore a camo baseball cap and snood. The latter can be drawn up over my face and is more comfortable than a head-net. Having picked my spot at the high edge of the hollow under an ivy overhang, I had a wait of an hour yet to sunset (if you could call it that on such day). I amused myself by picking off a few transitory woodpigeons as they floated in to land on the high branches. The main troop, the roost residents, would flock in later.

As the temperature descended I stood from time to time to restore the circulation in my legs and slid a disposable hand-warmer into the back of each shooting mitten to keep my hands comfortable. A few of these small packs, bought from an army surplus store, are always in my game-bag during winter. Keeping the trigger finger supple is crucial and a frozen shooter is a poor shooter.

As ever, the other creatures in the pit kept me amused during my watch. A robin mothered around, finding my intrusion impudent, as did a pair of Jenny-wrens. Both species are often seen around evergreen climbers like ivy and mistletoe.

The odd crow drifted over the pit and their alighting paid compliment to my concealment, though I fought back the temptation to shoot. With three plump pigeons in the bag already, my mind was centred on the 'edible'.

Scavenging rat

Until, that was, the piping of a dismayed blackbird warned me of a more ugly vermin close by. Following the outcry of the bird, my eye was drawn to a huge doe rat scavenging at the side of the pit, and heading in my direction. I consider rats foul creatures, not due to their appearance, but for the menace of disease they bear. The shot was instinctive and lethal. The noise of clattering wings from above as the rat rolled down into the pit reminded me

When the roost is settling, it's time to start picking off your targets

how stealthy the landing woodpigeon can often be. A dozen birds must have stolen in without my knowledge. Then, it was back to the wait, but with half an eye on the rat lair.

Soon the pigeons started to arrive in numbers and proceedings warmed up. The whirring of wings and the shadows thrown across a dim but lowering sun put me on the alert. Roost-borne birds circled to alight into the imperceptible wind. They dropped on open boughs to appraise the scene before fluttering into heavier cover. I noted where they flew, knowing they would bustle and preen before steadying down. I always baulk at shooting for a while, opting to wait for the numbers to increase. With many now at roost, I started to pick off birds at the moment they landed.

A well-placed shot beneath the tuck of the wing while they are outstretched will find the engine room: the heart or lungs. A pellet between the shoulder blades, if the back is presented, will achieve the same. Both shots will be terminal and are far more practical than the headshot advocated by many so-called 'experts'. The bobbing head of the woodpigeon is a difficult target but it sits upon a static body.

Need to understand anatomy

I choose the easy option. You will read many articles saying that the legal-limit air rifle isn't powerful enough to breech the armoured breastbone of the woodpigeon. A legal limit air rifle hits its target with around 3 ft/lbs of latent energy at 30 yards – enough to crack the skull of a rabbit and squirrel, so certain of dispatching a woodpigeon. If you shoot with an FAC air rifle then the heart/lung shot is definitely powerful enough. All of which brings me to a relevant point for the novice hunter. Anatomy may have been wearisome at school. To the vermin shooter it is crucial knowledge, whatever your quarry. Study well and you will despatch quarry cleanly.

Each shot from my air rifle, innocuous and almost unheard, is punctuated by the thud of a victim *hitting the deck*, alerting the roosters. Some will rustle and shuffle, some will fly off to circle and come back in again, others will flee. As the light fades, more stay than go. Unless a bird is pricked – and it happens – I leave them where they lie to collect at the end of the session.

On a brighter evening, I keep the sunset at my back so that the birds find me hard to spot and my scope won't reflect the light. I won't ever produce a shot-gunner's bag but a dozen plump breasts for the freezer is ample and that is all I will take: the breasts. I often dress out in the field and leave the rest of the carcases for the fox and the badger.

Today's session took eight birds out of the food chain. Not a massive result for my farmer but every little helps. Eventually, bad light stopped play and while I was cleaning out the breasts in the gloom, I could hear the scurry of rats in the undergrowth. It looked likely that Brer Fox would not get to the table in time tonight.

The silent rifle is an effective tool for roost shooting

It was cold now and I still had those tricky clay furrows to negotiate. No matter: it had been a fruitful session. A warm house beckoned and there was whisky in the jar.

The learning curve

Chicken and egg. Egg and chicken. How do you learn the way of bird and beast, how do you learn how to hunt, how do you learn how to shoot a rifle accurately, how do you choose the gun, what ammunition is best? Trial and error? Well, sometimes you learn quickly that way but the error can be either expensive or dangerous. Ideally, your apprenticeship is served at the coat-tails of men and women who have been 'in-country' all their lives. But what if, like me as a youngster, you didn't have access to such hands-on knowledge? Luckily, many of these folk have left us a legacy in the written word. In latter times, we have the benefit of modern media too, with a wealth of information and tuition available in DVD and video format. For me, books avidly devoured in my youth and still my staple diet, were the key to gaining theoretical wisdom.

Learning in the early days

As a youngster I started with factual books, poring over them and trying to build up an encyclopaedic memory. Bird and egg identification books, anything I could lay my hands on. Field trips would see me memorising birds: plumage, habitats, flight patterns, nests — then rushing home to pin a name on them. A juvenile twitcher, ticking off lists. I had huge tomes such as the *Reader's Digest Book of British Birds* and small pocket books — does anyone remember those little *Observer* books? How I wish I'd kept them all.

In those days, as a boy, egg collections were common and I was naïve enough to put ambition before conscience. The pursuit of collector's items was, I suppose, my first introduction to hunting. Watching a bird for hours, foraging in the hedgerow for its nest or climbing a tall pine (at risk to life and limb) and the achievement when I took my prize; the feeling wasn't dissimilar to the buzz I get now from a successful stalk.

Looking back, I'm not proud of what I did then but I learned a heck of a lot about British birds, a knowledge that would stay with me for life and serve me later when I turned to the gun and camera. Over the years I gathered books about mammals, flora, trees, tracks and trails — even the weather.

Influential writers

By now I was hunting and wanted to know everything I could that would give me advantage. My library started to extend into biographies and historical accounts of country lore. Richard Jeffries' nineteenth century accounts on gamekeepers and poachers, Jones & Woodward's *Gamekeeper's Notebook*, Ian Niall's *Poacher's Handbook*, all are packed with hints and tips from a bygone age but also (at times) stacked with country myth and mis-information. Though I've never been a wildfowler, I was absorbed by BB's (Denys Watkins-Pitchford's) romantic accounts of the wild foreshore, the rural landscape and by his iconic style of writing — chapters pulling you into the cold huddle of a dyke and forcing you to smell the ozone, feel the bite of the wind and hear the plaintive cry of fowl. Perhaps sitting in a barn watching swallows or watching the winter fox padding through the snowbound copse.

I also read everything I could about hunting dogs and their handlers. Brian Plummer's anthologies about lurchers and terriers, and the rascals or rogues he encountered, enthralled me. Indeed, his *Complete Lurcher* and Jackie Drakeford's works on lurcher training were responsible for making Dylan (my Bedlington cross lurcher) the worthwhile companion he is today — though Plummer would turn in his grave, and Jackie would disapprove, I'm

Want to learn?
Then keep a library of reference books

the reader. It's all knowledge, generously imparted.

Game cookery books

I have always believed in eating, where possible, what I shoot so I have a range of cookery books too. The late, great Fred Taylor instructed me, through his *One For The Pot,* how to prepare my first rabbits and hares. Very tasty they were too! He shares a section in my modest library with others: Prue Coats, Angela Humphreys, Whittingstall, Paterson/McKelvie and that irreverent old scoundrel, Willie Fowler. His tongue-in-cheek recipe for cormorant has to be an all-time classic.

Shooting magazines

Perhaps one of the easiest sources for direct learning is the shooting magazine. Up-to-the-minute, topical, seasonal and pictorial. There are many good contributors in the shooting press – and some bad ones, too. There is a vast difference between magazine articles and books, however. The magazine editor has tight deadlines, target subjects and a budget to meet. They want inventive pictures and stark, factual content: they generally haven't the space for colourful, flowing prose and descriptive essays. But for the student 'in a hurry' they are a rich source of learning.

Even videos...

While the visual media have their place, they're not really for me. I do have a few DVDs by experts such as: John Darling,

sure, at my insistence on using a gazehound cross as a gundog. In this modern era, there are books published frequently about hunting in all its forms and nearly every author can guarantee at least one reader: me – for I can never resist.

The late John Darling's works on the airgun influenced me greatly. Jim Tylers manuals, Pete Wadesons ultimate work on the subject and lately John Bezzant's offering. If only I had had them all on my bookshelf thirty years ago, the journey would have been so much easier.

There are many other authors too and a range of subjects. John Humphreys on pigeons, Sean Frain on rabbits, rats and foxes, Fred J Taylor, Richard Brigham. The list is immense and all have a hint or a tip or an experience to share with and The Warrener etc. Very good they are too and their growing popularity shows they obviously have a market. I have also watched some dreadful offerings. Amateurish, inaccurate and staged. No, give me a good book or a magazine over these every time. A cold November night, a warm chair, an interesting read and a dram. Any author who can draw me out there alongside them into the countryside, and teaches me a little something along the way, gets my vote every time.

All of this, of course, will only take you part of the way on your quest for knowledge. The full apprenticeship is served out in 'real-time', whether training a dog, stalking a rabbit or skulking in a hide watching the wary magpie.

There is no better way to learn than through real observation

Weather... what weather?

I have no idea where the hunting genes flowing through my blood were spawned. Certainly not my father or his father before him. Confinement indoors sees me prowling like a caged lion, a trait I share with my dog. Perhaps that's why I picked a lurcher as a canine companion? We both live to be out hunting. We both have to have our regular 'fix'. It amuses me that many hunters put away the rifle during unsettled weather. I have to hunt all year round, I just can't do 'seasons'. It helps that I've made sure I've secured the right kinds of permission, the right facilities and the right clothing to ensure I can get out and hunt whatever conditions Mother Nature throws at me. The shooting hardware we use nowadays is robust and can endure anything the British weather can throw at it, provided (of course) we know about aftercare. More on that later.

Different conditions, even severe weather, can open up new hunting opportunities. You just need to know your quarry intimately, have respect and knowledge of local landscape and meteorological patterns and look at the various conditions and the chances they can offer.

Shooting hardware is robust – it just needs aftercare in conditions like this

Shooting in the rain

Rain, for example? There is a huge difference, particularly in comfort levels, between the humid summer thunderstorm and the icy stair-rods of a November squall. Sheltering beneath the broad canopy of a beech copse, watching the lightning (ignoring all those warnings about not standing beneath trees) can be quite invigorating. It will put you back in touch with the drama of nature. If you have your wits about you and know your land intimately, it also gives you an opportunity for vermin control.

Birds and animals will warn you of an impending storm. Bug-eaters like swallows or swifts will swoop in low following the flies and midges that have been pushed down by the air pressure. When you see this happening, seek the shelter of the wood quickly . You'll be there before the pigeons and the corvids, who will be looking to roost before the storm breaks.

Storm shooting

Settle in a dark niche under a beech or conifer and ride out the storm. Under the right tree you'll barely get wet, trust me. Trees and lightning? Yes, I know, but there is probably more chance of being knocked down by a bus while shopping in town. The solitary tree in an open landscape isn't a good idea, but the wood should be safe. Life is too short to miss the awesome spectacle of a good storm. You will be in a prime position to target those birds flying in to take roost.

Then, when the storm has passed by, there are more opportunities to take. Those roosting birds will flap and fluster,

190

drying off their feathers and giving away their location. The coneys who went deep into their burrows long, long before you guessed the rain was coming, now steal back out to lick the droplets from leaf stems. The wet woodland floor will make for silent progress as you stalk toward the warren. I love the summer rain. A good camouflaged rain-top and baseball cap are all I need. When I get home, I'll wipe the gun with a towel and leave it for a while to dry naturally, scope covers open to let the lenses dry too. A rub down with gun oil before the rifle goes back into the safe will stop any rust setting in.

Freezing winter squalls are an entirely different prospect. A drenching in cold conditions will drive down your core body temperature, which can quickly reduce shooting efficiency. You won't want to stay long in the open, particularly if the wind is keen, when hypothermia becomes a real threat. You don't have to hide away indoors, though. This is the time to find some indoor shooting, or to at least find an indoor sniping point. There are jackdaws and feral pigeons to be cleared from their roosts in the barns and cattle sheds. Rats will be raiding the silos and feed stores. A shadowy corner inside the farm buildings will give the opportunity to surprise unwary quarry and give good sport.

What about real cold snaps and hard frosts? You would do well to remember the old adage: 'Hard times make for hard measures'. This rings true as much for wildlife as for us. The primeval drive for

basic sustenance will cause many wild creatures, normally cautious, to take risks. The natural inclination to vigilance and prudence will often be over-ridden by a hungry beast. One survival trait all living things have in common, including man, is that starvation means death.

For this simple reason, even in the coldest weather, hunting opportunities will still be found. Many air rifle quarry species will be at their most vulnerable. Some hunters may consider this 'unsporting', but if vermin control is your objective and if your permission to shoot on land relies on results, then consider this: those same species have all the advantage in times of abundance. Personally, I consider it quite 'unsporting' for a hundred rabbits to hide all summer chomping away, out of sight and out of range of my gun, in the middle of a two acre maize crop! Nature has a way of restoring the balance, I hope you'll agree?

Set out with the rifle after a crisp hoar frost and you'll find it very difficult to stalk those desperate creatures that venture out to feed in sub-zero temperatures. Conditions underfoot will be crisp and unforgiving and every footfall will crack and echo around the copse or wood. The meadow is adorned with silver, rimy cobwebs spread like a huge gossamer blanket. A beautiful sight to behold, but no hunting ground.

Hole-up in the deep cover of the thicket for a while, wrapped in thermals, and eventually some of your quarry will come to you. Pigeons will be easy to spot at roost in the bare branches, silhouetted against the grey sky. Squirrels may well venture out to delve but will struggle to reach their caches of nuts and beech mast, the ground being so hard set. I, though, will have bait down, both beech mast and acorns gathered in autumn and kept for just such a day. Crows and magpies will be desperate, so I will have eggs and dog food in my bag too.

Tracking in the snow

One of life's delights, to me, is walking out into an inch or two of virgin snow. Stepping out with both gun and dog doubles the pleasure. To watch my lurcher ease out of the door, bury his long nose into the white stuff, snort, sniff and throw it up into the air then chase around maniacally, is a celebration of true winter. Sadly, in this era of 'global warming', I can count on two hands the number of occasions this has happened during his six years out here in Norfolk.

Snowfall is my cue to go track-reading. Blizzard conditions, the proverbial 'white-out', are obviously a no-go. Once the snow is down, however, the opportunity is there to hone up on fieldcraft skills. Track-reading on snow-covered land will give you a real insight into your shooting land.

Unlike any other season, you won't merely chance across the odd footprint at a muddy puddle; you will often find a complete trail from a quarry's home to its feeding point, from its hiding place to its kill. Fox, badger, deer, rabbit, stoat,

A fox has leapt from the ditch and pounced on a rabbit

weasel, rat, squirrel, mink: their suspected presence will be proven. More importantly, they will lay tracks on their regular paths that you will remember long after the snow has melted. You will find trails leading to rat lairs and rabbit burrows that you never knew existed. Hunting quarry is still possible, but little will pass in front of your muzzle.

Caution when hunting in fog

Hunting in a cold, damp winter fog can be a very eerie experience. Heavy fog throws a blanket over both sound and scent. I once walked right into a small herd of roe deer in fog, spooking them so much that one tried to charge me. So stalking can be fruitful, but you need to take special care. If visibility is reduced to less than a hundred yards you will need to be very conscious of backstops.

Do you have livestock on your land? Do you know where they are feeding today? Where are the buildings? Do you know where footpaths are? Shooting without a known backstop is irresponsible at any time. If I stalk rabbits in fog, I shoot from a standing position so that the ground itself will stop any stray pellets.

Often, it's better to stick to woodland stalking where the natural heat emitted from the tree trunks prevents a dense fog from descending to ground level. A fog hangs over a wood in the same way as over a town or over street lights. A white mist swirling above the trees will highlight roosting birds such as woodpigeons or corvids. In fact, woodies will sit tight in dense fog, reluctant to fly, even when you are walking quietly underneath them. Take advantage of this.

No sport in a gale
Quite simply, forget airgun hunting outdoors in gale conditions. Make sure your permitted hunting ground includes storage barns and cattle sheds, though, and you can enjoy some feral pigeon or rat control. High winds often alter the landscape of your shooting grounds. Weak, unstable trees will have toppled and can supply you with new hides or cover,

particularly if they're covered in ivy. Take the opportunity to explore them. Look for bird's nests in the ivy and try to understand which species were nesting there. If the windfalls contained squirrel dreys, open one up and examine it. Learn about your quarry. Where did it get the horsehair? Now you know to watch the stable block before the next brood.

Heatwave conditions
Slogging around your shoot when temperatures are soaring can be hot, thirsty work and it looks like something we're going to have get used to, if climate change predictions are correct. Quarry will be abundant, especially near to water sources. Ponds, streams and water tanks will be magnets for corvids and pigeons but they will also attract swarms of midges, the hunter's bane. During long droughts there is another nuisance for the woodland stalker. Trees will slough their leaves as though autumn has arrived but without any rain, the floor is like a cornflake bowl without the milk.

Hunting is best done at the crack of dawn, when the heat-mists have dampened the leaves underfoot and your quarry will be feeding (and watering) before the onslaught of the summer sun. Mid-day will be for the proverbial *mad-dogs and Englishmen* (no co-incidence then that I have a crazy dog and I live in Norfolk?) but dusk, when the mist descends again, will see vermin back on the move.

Breast practise

Most game cookery books will include recipes for one of Britain's staple shooting quarries: the woodpigeon. So why do so many of these plump, table-friendly birds end up left cast into some ditch simply because the shooter doesn't want the hassle of preparing his catch? Or just doesn't know how?

Plucking and drawing a pigeon so that it will sit on a plate like a Sunday roast chicken ready for the carving knife seems hardly worth the effort. When I stare at a plucked pigeon with its coat off, I sympathise with that view.

There is, however, a much easier way of gleaning the best meat from the humble woodpigeon and it takes less than five minutes per bird. The most versatile and succulent meat worth taking from the shot pigeon is from its ample breast. Each side of the bird's deep breastbone holds a rich 'escalope' of dark, rich meat which lends itself to preparation in kebabs, pies, stir-fries, curries, paté's or a simple pan-fried snack. There are recipes for this elsewhere, so I will just tell you how to gather this meat for the freezer. Forget the rest of the bird. Let's concentrate on the breasts, as the actress said to the bishop.

So, why would preparation be full of 'hassle'? Well, mainly, it will be the

Plucking a pigeon under the tap in the sink keeps the feathers in one spot

Cut out the two breasts taking care not to pierce the crop

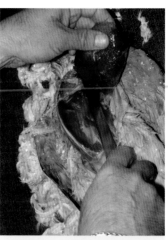

The only meat really worth keeping on a pigeon is the breast

feathers. You've all done it, I'm sure: spread the bird on the kitchen cutting board, start plucking feathers and a breeze gusts through the window or someone opens the door. The draught blows the feathers everywhere! Do this once and you'll regret it. Worse still, do it while the wife is watching and you'll think, 'Never again!'

There are simple solutions, I promise. The first is to breast out in the field and leave discarded feathers and carcase in the hedgerow. Fox or rat territory preferred. This isn't always practical or possible. Don't worry though. Take the birds home. Try the following, then put your family to the 'feather test'!

This was shown to me by a shooting man who has spent a lifetime hiding his hunting sins from his family (and particularly from his wife). My father-in-law!

Choose a quiet moment (i.e. no around to catch you) and allow five minutes per pigeon. Lay the bird on its back in the kitchen sink and run the cold water tap on it while working. It's also useful to have one of those filter things in the drain. Lift the bird and break back the wings at the joints. Soak the outside of the breast feathers while taking time to admire their watertight properties. Ruffle your fingers into the feathers, under the running water, lifting the downy feathers to wet them underneath. You will note that they're not so watertight now and will understand why the roosting pigeon faces the driving rain.

Keeping the tap running and firmly pluck away the down, drenching each handful under the tap. Drop the wet feathers into the sink. When the breast is clear, use a fillet knife to nick the skin above the centre of the breastbone. Then peel the skin right back on either side to the wing joints. This exposes the whole of the dark, red breast meat. Using the fillet knife, pare out these twin medallions one at a time. Cut down from the breast bone, following the line of the cartilage down, round and out toward the wing on each side.

Take care, as you slide the blade out toward to the wing joint, not to nick the crop. This will definitely give the game away as it will leave a pungent aroma in the kitchen for the discerning nose to later use to accuse you. Avoid this error and inside

five minutes, you can drop two of nature's most rich, succulent offerings of meat into the strainer. Wash them thoroughly, pat them dry with kitchen towel and put them into a freezer bag. You'll need to place 4 to 6 in the freezer bag for a decent meal.

The soaked feathers can be scooped up from the sink and thrown into a doubled-up carrier bag with the rest of the carcase. Tie it firmly (as you would your roast chicken carcase) and lose it in the bin.

There shouldn't be a feather in sight, nor any aroma. If there is, your family will soon let you know!

December

Squirrel Hunt

Through leafless wood and copse, they check the dreys
And search the forest floor for sign of greys.
The scuffled mulch, the delve, the cache revealed
Broken kernels, rotting acorns peeled.
The sign is fresh, the quarry must be near
They settle into cover, purpose clear.
The lurcher sniffs the breeze, he raises paw
He has the scent and hears the scrabbling claw.
The Hunter scans the trees nearby and, look!
A fluffy tail trailing from a nook.
A well-placed pellet smacks a nearby bough,
The squirrel quickly bolts and leaps and now
It crawls behind a trunk, to Hunter blind.
In walks the patient dog, his task in mind.
The Hunter raises gun and signals hound
The lurcher scratches trunk and works around.
At fear of dog, the grey comes back in view
The rifle spits, the Hunter's mark hits true.
The dog, his work unfinished, below stands
To catch the falling grey before it lands.

Foragers and fools

I mentioned elsewhere nature's abhorrence of a vacuum. There is no better demonstration of this theory than grey squirrel management. Unless you have total control of a vast area of land, elimination is impossible and that's probably no bad thing. I hold the same view on squirrels as I do on rabbits. Alien, it may well be, but it is now a fixture on the British fauna list and part of the food chain. Annihilation of the grey squirrel would be a sad affair and if control wasn't needed, you and I would have one less excuse to be in a wood with a gun. I can fully understand the ruthless pogroms against this rodent in areas where red squirrel breeding programmes are underway. I've never seen a red squirrel in the Norfolk area I shoot, though older locals assure me it was prolific here in their youth. Nor will I ever see them breed here in my lifetime.

Grey squirrel culling
Where I have permission to shoot grey squirrels, I do so without guilt. As often as I clear an area, they return within months. I could, if I were the worrying type, lie in my bed imagining all those little greys

Waiting for incomers

scurrying across from the neighbouring wood (where I have no shooting rights) and surveying all the abandoned dreys as I toss and turn. They tear down the 'For Let' signs and move in, uninvited squatters licking their lips at the prospect of hazelnuts, maize cobs, and all those eggs or chicks whose return I've encouraged. But I don't worry, I'll be up and out with my gun next morning anyhow. Issuing eviction orders.

Mid-winter is a prime time to cull grey squirrels, for three reasons. Forget any nonsense you read about hibernation. Dormice hibernate, squirrels just slow down their activity. They will be as lively as ever when they're out of the drey; they just appear less frequently. They will be out and about, in sunshine or snow, digging out the caches of food buried in the mulch of the woodland floor.

That is the first reason for targeting them at this time of year. Spot these excavations on the floor – easy to see – and

Foraging signs on the woodland floor

will use that natural ace card played by the female of almost every species: she has what he wants but isn't prepared to give it up easily! I say 'almost' because the vixen, at this time of year, is playing the opposite game and screaming 'come and get me!'. But the result of the squirrel's 'play hard to get' regime is that, at times, the woodland floor and tree-trunks are a flurry of activity as males chase females. Now as we all know, there is nothing so foolish, so distracted, so single-mindedly focused and so vulnerable as the testosterone-fuelled male of the species with half a chance of mating. Any species!

So, this morning, deliberately chosen after consulting the oracle (my weather clock) Dylan and I are about to engage in his favourite activity. The gestation period for a female squirrel is about a month and a half. They will give birth between February and March, first brood. A hoar frost morning is not the time to cull greys, particularly if it is one of a series. The ground is too hard for their foraging. They won't be attempting to break open autumn's hidden food. The leaves and detritus on the forest floor will be hard and will crackle underfoot. Your progress will be like a mother at a children's birthday party, treading frustratedly across a carpet of potato crisps.

watch them carefully. A foraging squirrel is relatively static and an easier target.

The second reason for culling now is the lack of cover in the tree-tops. Fairly obvious really, but the squirrel is easier to spot and follow silhouetted between dark, bare branch and grey sky. Getting it to stop long enough for a shot is another art but more on that later.

The third and final reason for adding squirrel to the quarry list in December is that, while other creatures (except, perhaps, for the fox) have their ardour frozen, the male squirrel has a twinkle in his eye. Unfortunately for him, his mate

Slight thaw brings out the squirrels
Today, though, a few days of winter sunshine have melted the frost. The mulch on the ground is soft and wet and the thaw has

opened up an opportunity for my quarry to dig, therefore feed. The females are in season. Perfect conditions. This is a hunting activity which will, without fail, include the lurcher and he's rolling about in anticipation as the gun goes into the slip. Until we reach the wood, Dylan has no idea what the game is today. He's in for a treat.

Lurcher loved squirrel-chasing

The Hunting Act, that ridiculous concoction of ill-informed legislation designed by fools with no knowledge of bird and beast but claiming their salvation, came at a bad time for my lurcher pup. Rescued from the potential restraint and conditions endured by his parents (chained to a caravan on a tinker site) he threw himself into my wife's arms, guaranteeing preservation, only to find himself the working companion of an air rifle hunter. With all the demands which that would bring. Silence (easy for

Winter is a fine time to thin out grey squirrels

a lurcher), total obedience (more difficult) and a restriction of his natural instinct, to chase, on most occasions. He adapted well, and the one free rein I allowed him was to chase squirrels, naively thinking that he'd never catch one anyway. At just nine months old, he caught his first and soon developed a knack for anticipating the sprint to a trunk, cutting off the escape route. As quickly as he had mastered this art, it was curtailed by a crowd of imbeciles in a decrepit old institution in a dirty, noisy city who had nothing on their minds but a scribbled cross on a ballot paper. Again, the pup adapted. Suddenly, called off the chase with a curt 'Leave!!' he was confused. In the hidden depths of dark copses in central Norfolk, as in my youth, I was tempted to ignore the law, for his sake. More mature now, I was aware that unless this discipline was instilled I ran the risk of losing my dog – and guns and vehicle – if he chanced upon a running squirrel on public land and in plain view of a hunting ban supporter.

Now re-trained to point and retrieve

So Dylan has learned to mark, point and retrieve the grey squirrel. It would be wonderful to think that by the time this book is published this audacious Act had been repealed and Dylan still had the legs on him to snatch up a running grey.

Today, restrictions aside, he loves this game. He will lie by my side under cover in the damp wood as we watch the wisps of mist evaporate from the floor. His long tongue hangs out, panting. His brown

201

eyes flash left and right, up and down. His ears wave up and down, forward and backward, independent of each other, radar dishes catching signals from deep within the spinney. His moist nose twitches, as a million receptors sense the musky odour

Rabbit damage on sugar beet

of squirrel. Suddenly, he sits up. The nose, eyes and ears all pointing in one direction. He glances at me, checking that I have the gun to my shoulder, and continues his vigil. As I watch through the scope, two greys appear – the mating chase. The dog is shaking, desperate to launch into a chase but stays at my whispered command and lies down. They get nearer, frolicking around the trunks. In range and the dog knows it, casting a frustrated glance at me again. I squeak loudly and the chase stops. One is on the ground, alert. The other is spread-eagled on a beech trunk just a foot from the ground, inviting the pellet

which ends the romance. As the other goes vertical, a scrabbling panic into the upper boughs, I release Dylan who runs in to check the kill and bring it back. A jay, the squirrel's mortal enemy, screams her delight and crashes through the wood.

Best she doesn't linger too long, with another pellet already in the breech.

We move on, watching for movement in the trees and on the floor. There are a series of feeding spots and highways I want to check: low stumps which have been covered in kernels in recent weeks, fallen saplings where I've seen squirrels treading the tight-rope as they traverse. The first stump bears fruit after a wait and a large male, pre-occupied with shelling a cob-nut, is next to fall. Further on, Dylan alerts me to movement and we drop to the floor behind a trunk. A younger, first-year grey scampers across a fallen bough. I click my tongue and it halts, alert. A fatal pause. The dog makes his third retrieve. It's going to be a fruitful day.

Vigilance

There are, of course, a many factors which contribute to success as an air rifle hunter. The right gun, robust ammunition, lots of range practise, camouflage clothing, well-placed hides and fieldcraft: all of these ingredients help to bake the pie that is an efficient vermin controller. Over the years I've talked to and had letters or e-mails from many new air rifle shooters who (having mixed the above ingredients) are still having trouble connecting with quarry. By that, I don't mean 'missing' shots. I mean not finding any quarry on their permission to shoot. The vital ingredient, the yeast that makes the pie rise, is vigilance.

One thing you should learn very quickly in the field is that even if you can't see them, wild creatures (who survive on their senses) will often see you and react accordingly. The good news, though, is that doesn't always mean they'll flee. Most small mammals have a natural inclination to freeze to avoid detection. Their in-bred instincts seem to tell them that movement means exposure.

Birds, on the other hand, tend to do the opposite, but they have the advantage of flight. Even so, many birds will hop swiftly into cover to watch any perceived threat first. Of course, the other advantage that most quarry species have is their own natural camouflage. What the would-be shooter needs to develop is a *'hunters eye'*. The ability to scan a hedgerow, a tree, a crop, any scene – and spot the unusual, the 'out-of-place'. This skill is something that only comes with practise and observation. There is a homework syllabus that the hunting scholar can take to short-cut the journey from blind novice to artisan. This can loosely be broken into four components: habitat, habit, outline and patience. Let's look at them in that order.

Watch the rabbit warren for a while before shooting

The magpie will spiral up into the crown, so be ready!

Habitat

While walking your shooting permission, pay attention to the types of habitat that exist there and look around for signs of occupation. The hedgerow: what types of shrubs make up the line? Hawthorn and blackthorn are both favourite haunts of magpies and jays. Elderberry and mistletoe will harbour woodpigeon, particularly when the berries are ripe. What about the base? Briars, nettles and gorse are worth checking for hidden rabbit burrows. Any dense cover, such as Old Man's Beard, will allow daytime rabbits to sit out.

Check the woodland and copses thoroughly. Get to know them like the back of your hand. Corvids and pigeons will gravitate to high boughs: trees where they can perch and scan for food or danger. Learn where the best cover is in relation to these vantage points. Learn, too, how to move toward them on a route which will keep you hidden. Even the smallest spinney can be, if not a haven, a stop-over for all manner of wildlife. Pass it by and it will be to your loss. I find these small coverts excellent for roost-shooting and pigeon decoying. Conifer plantations will invariably house grey squirrels and jays.

Soil type is also a good indicator of likely vermin presence. Rabbits will avoid thick clay (for obvious reasons) and also damp, peaty soil. They will thrive in loamy, sandy soils where they can delve deep into the landscape. Rats, on the other hand, love damp and dank conditions.

Look for co-habitation. The fox earth and the badger sett only exist where there will be plentiful food and that usually means rabbits. The same applies to the stoat and weasel.

Crops are the magnet that gives you, the airgunner, license to shoot vermin. Spend some time studying them. Learn when they are likely to be drilled, which creatures will target them as they ripen and when they will be harvested, for this is often a bumper time for control. As the crop grows, its natural raiders have hide-outs close by; burrows, lairs, roosts, dreys and nests. Find them. Hide up close by and ambush them. At seed and early-growing stage, every creature on the General

License will attack crops. Mature barley will attract rabbits and rats. Brassicas will draw in rabbits and woodpigeon. Ripe maize (sweetcorn) will pull in squirrels, woodpigeon and crows but the coneys won't ignore them either. Sugarbeet tubers are nectar to rabbits and the broad leaf above gives ideal cover for a hungry largo-morph.

Don't forget the farmyard. Study it carefully and find the clues to its raiders. Rat spoor, pigeon droppings, the cast feather of a magpie. Study the footprints in the mud. Open pig fields will draw vermin from miles around: rats and corvids partic-ularly. All year round, the farmyard will be visited by many opportunistic animals and birds. So, too, will the disused factory or the refuse tip.

Learn the habits of your quarry

The routines of every creature make it vulnerable to predation. Returning to an abundant food source, perching at the same look-out point, roosting overnight in the same tree, drinking at the same pool, following the same exit trail from a lair or burrow. If you see the freshly gnawed kernel of sweetcorn lying on the grass by the maize crop, hide away patiently and wait. The squirrel is either in there getting more or will come back from the wood to get some soon. It will bring the cob to the margin again where it can turn it freely between its paws. Watch a rabbit warren for some time before you shoot there. Let the rabbits come and go and learn the runs.

Even magpies have a 'trail' they follow through the wood or along the hedgerow. Study it and anticipate where they will perch next. Be ready with the gun. Watch the magpie approach the base of a tall tree. It will spiral up, round the trunk, through the branches and emerge at the top. Train your scope up there before it reaches the crown.

Find the drinking spots. Every living creature needs water. Ponds, water troughs, streams, puddles: all will attract passing vermin. Even scavengers like the crow or woodpigeon can't resist the odd splash around in a shallow pool. Rats, of course, are never far from water. There are two of your quarry, though, who dislike getting their feet wet. The rabbit will take its drink from the dew on the meadow grass or from the small puddles left in the base of a broad-leafed plant such as dock or rhubarb. Remember this after an early morning rain-shower. Similarly, the squirrel will drink at the 'well' formed in the cleft of a tree and will come back frequently.

Some vermin have seasonal habits which the hunter will remember and exploit. The need to mate is one of the dominant habits. Squirrels chasing around the wood in November and March will be exposed and pre-occupied. Corvids nest-building and courting during March, April and May are at their most vulnerable.

There are others which are less conspic-uous. The rat colony moving from the farm buildings to the hedgerow alongside the barley field, their summer lodgings, the ears of grain dropping from the ripening barley stalks being the attraction. The hatching of crane flies in the September meadow grass will have jackdaws and magpies waltzing around as they chase the succulent 'daddy-long-legs'. The pond-skaters hatching in the water troughs under the warm June sun will see the magpies fishing from the edge. The outbreak of May bugs on the meadow (usually a two-yearly event) will make it worth hiding up in the adjacent wood to catch the jays, who find them irresistible, hopping around like young farmers at a barn dance.

You will spot other behaviour and routines that will increase shooting efficiency: the fact that a woodpigeon will land into the breeze, wings outstretched, giving a brief moment of exposure; the tendency of the rabbit to pause momen-tarily outside its burrow when fleeing danger. This is a shooting opportunity, but you'd better be accurate or it will flip into the hole instinctively if injured.

The rats tendency toward cannibalism. Don't collect shot rats: leave them for a while and watch their greedy brethren come back to the scent of spilt blood. Then shoot them too.

The reaction of rabbits to a gunlamp. Some will squat down, some will run. Leave the squatters and play the light in front of the runners. They will often stop dead, reluctant to cross the beam. Shoot and repeat. Then play the beam back to the squatters. They thought they'd escaped your attention. There are dozens of little tricks and traits based on the behaviour of our quarry that you will remember in the field. Too many to write here.

Learn to recognise your quarry by its profile

The silhouettes of your quarry

The more intimately you get to know the land on which you shoot, the easier it becomes to spot the unusual. Yet, in order to understand what is unusual, you need to learn how to identify quarry (or even parts of quarry) at a glance.

Even from a legal viewpoint, it is a wise shooter who learns how to recognise his quarry's silhouette, even its flight or movement, before venturing a shot. It's this 'instant recognition' that can change the quarry count significantly. It's not something that can be taught, it's something that needs to be learned the hard way. Only hours of observation will give you this skill. How can I describe it?

I can often spot the translucent ear tips of a wary rabbit among the tall nettles in a hedgerow. How? Because I've trained my eye to search for aberrations in a scene. The huddled form under a twilight bush, looking like a rock? It wasn't there last time I passed. Through the scope, the glint of an eye betrays the rabbit. The dark, motionless clump on a sparse bough, is conspicuous against a grey skyline. Should it be there? Again, the magnification and light-capture of the riflescope shows detail and the squirrel drops to the woodland floor with a thud.

The flash of iridescent pink or violet that catches my eye against the green canopy of a summer copse. The sight picture in the scope, gently raised so as not to return the wink, marks the pigeons kill-zone.

The slightly stuttered flight of a bird into the stark limbs of a winter oak, the lowering sun blinding my eyes. An instant decision before she lands. If she perches horizontally, she risks death. The bird lands upright, head above tail, so I stay the

Observation is the cornerstone of successful hunting

shot. I raise the scope, expecting to see a green woodpecker. At the glint of the sun on my lens, a harsh shriek and the jay escapes. At least I didn't make a mistake – and never have, in thirty years. Had she perched with her head in line with her tail, she would be dead. For that's how a jay normally lands.

The outline of the magpie is distinctive due its long tail, but could you tell a carrion crow from a rook in silhouette? Both are on the General License so perhaps it won't matter to you, but what if your landowner insists you leave the rooks alone? There are still estates that believe the loss of a rookery is a harbinger of poor fortune, so shooting them is taboo. The seasoned hunter will recognise the outline immediately. They will look to the beak and the legs. A slender, pointed beak and plus-fours around the knees is the rook. A stout beak and skinny, exposed legs is the crow.

The dove family are much more difficult if you can't see plumage. The outline of the collared dove is more slender than the woodpigeon but the woodie and the turtle dove are similar in profile. Be careful, for shooting the latter could see you prosecuted. It is protected. If in doubt, don't shoot. As with the crow and rook, however, you may be able to gauge identity by numbers. Turtle doves will be found in pairs only. If there are numerous huddled forms on the boughs, it's a safe bet you're looking at roosting woodpigeons.

Mammals are easier. Learn the outline of rabbit against hare. The ears have it. A coneys ears are the same length as its head. The hare's are half that again. If you're near water, think twice about the dark brown form that you've decided is a rat. Water voles are few and far between nowadays so please don't shoot one mistakenly. Again, look to the ears but also the tail. The rat's tail will be at least equal to its body length, if not longer. The voles is more stunted. The rat's ears will show. The water voles won't.

If you see a long, slinky, agitated form, don't worry about what species it is unless you're North of the Border. Stoat, weasel, mink, they're all murderous little tykes, deserving of a shot. Up North, however,

you may be looking at a pine marten. Leave it alone unless you're sure.

The hunter's patience

Patience may be a virtue, but it's an absolute necessity for the hunter. Many of the people who contact me complaining about failure to connect with quarry are probably guilty of impatience. The seasoned hunter learns to move gently and stealthily through the countryside, blending with the form and shadow of the landscape, staying in harmony with the scene around him. He will pause often and for long periods, knowing that haste and sudden movement will drive the watching creatures before him. In the wood, the hunter will scan the floor before him for a silent path, free of twigs and leaf litter. He will take four or five steps, pause and study the scene around him, listening for movement, watching for disturbance, then move on slowly again. This gentle progress will bring him quietly to his destination.

He will settle under cover, arrange his kit and wait. As long as it takes. Within 15 minutes the wood will forget the hunter's presence. Birds will fuss about, squirrels and rabbits will return to the pressing business of finding food and the hunter's opportunity will come.

This new-found discipline will be extended to the act of shooting itself. The adrenalin that precedes a shot needs to be controlled. The hunter doesn't rush, but he doesn't procrastinate either. Quarry species won't hang around long. If the shot looks difficult and despatch can't be guaranteed, let the quarry pass by. The hunter will get other chances but knows that if he takes the shot and misses, even with an air rifle, he will need to let the habitat settle down all over again.

And you? Sit back quietly, let yourself adjust to the sounds and sights around you. Develop your senses. Your ear will learn to recognise signals that quarry is approaching: the chacking of the magpie, the scramble of the squirrels paws on a tree trunk, the rustle of the leaf bed under the loping rabbit. Your eyes will catch the slightest movement: the flutter of a wing or the flick of a tail, the high bough bending under weight, the shadow thrown across the floor.

Before you qualify as a hunter, you must serve an apprenticeship as an observer. That will mean returning home from many outings with an empty bag, but with a growing wealth of knowledge. Trust me, hunting is an art: your quarry will rarely throw itself in front of your muzzle asking to be shot. Think about it for a moment. If it was that easy, it wouldn't be called hunting. It would simply be called 'shooting'.

Reality check

The shooting press sometimes displays an apparent reluctance to report on the fact that, sometimes, quarry are injured rather than cleanly killed. Though I expected to see the article rejected, I was grateful when *Sporting Rifle* were bold enough to print a treatise by me on this subject. I'm sure none of us is in total denial, but it sometimes seems that admitting to injuring (rather than cleanly dispatching) quarry seems completely taboo. Yet it happens, so let's just admit it. The reason I wrote on the subject, however, was because of the absence of constructive advice to the newcomer who, faced with an injured bird or animal, may find the situation so distressing that they may put down the gun for good.

I have always advocated the need to be very selective with shots using an air rifle. It is a highly efficient gun in qualified hands, but a total disaster in un-practised ones. I'm not about to lecture about quarry kill-zones. There is plenty of advice by other authors, in books, in monthly magazines and on the internet about this subject (though I will mention a few of my prefer-ences!) Quite simply, the quickest way to bring about the swift death of any small vermin is to place a pellet in the brain or heart. If you don't know where these organs are on a creature, you need to learn before you attempt a shot at that quarry. If you're not prepared to take the time to do that, sell your rifle and take up kite-flying or some other harmless past-time.

So, you've kept your air rifle. Hopefully, you've shot at inanimate targets across varying ranges and in different conditions for months to familiarise yourself with

Necking a rabbit – if you can't face this, don't hunt

both the weapon and its ammunition. Now, you feel confident enough to test yourself against live quarry. That confidence, with an air rifle, requires that you can place a tiny pellet into a 25mm circle at distances from 10 to 40 paces consistently. Not rarely. Consistently.

Wounding your quarry

Despite many years of experience I will (just like the deer stalker, the pigeon decoyer and the high-bird game shooter) occasionally think I've placed the terminal shot, only to find that my quarry is limping or flapping away. Or perhaps lying twitching pathetically. This is, to the true hunter, a calamity, but one that you need to get used

to, for an injured creature is often vocal in its distress. This scenario is one which will severely test your nerves. Your conscience implores you to react and dispatch swiftly. Any person who could ignore such distress (vermin or not) is not worthy to carry a gun. There are many anti-shooting types who consider the shooting of a creature 'cruel'. They mis-use the word. Cruelty is to abuse and to inflict prolonged pain. Shooting, correctly done, does no such thing. If incorrectly done, however, it will. The old adage about putting something 'out of its misery' was coined for a reason.

Back to the airgun. You will be faced with many different situations and each will be unique. I can only offer advice on those I've encountered. Let's take it quarry by quarry, remembering that I'm only talking about airgun hunting here.

Head shot for rabbits

When rabbit shooting I prefer the head shot above all else. A .22 pellet between the eye and ear is usually effective. To the new gun, the sight of a rabbit flipping and twitching after such a shot may be disturbing. Rest assured that the lights are out; it's just the engine room shutting down. Get used to it. This nervous reaction will often cause a coney to flip into the nearest hole so always shoot when it's well clear of the burrows. However, if the rabbit squeals, move in quickly.

Remember, your gun has two zeros, primary and secondary. If you move closer than the primary (10 / 11 yard) zero you will find the shot difficult unless you've practiced shooting below this distance. Keep 10 yards away and aim for a heart/lung shot. If this isn't possible (i.e. the rabbit is hidden under foliage) get right up to it.

You should now look for a manual solution. The ferreter's dispatch. Grab the rabbit simultaneously around the throat with one hand and by the back legs with the other. Stretch the rabbit's spine swiftly, cracking back the neck at the same time with your thumb beneath the rabbit's jaw. Job done.

If you're unfortunate and the coney has managed to flip into a burrow, be cautious. There are writers who advocate simply reaching into the burrow to pull it out. I certainly do, but I now wear light

Learning the art of clean dispatch is essential

gardening gloves carried in my game bag. Once stricken, twice shy. I still carry a scar on my hand where, a few years back, I attempted to drag what I thought was a dead rabbit from a blind bury. As I grabbed the paws, the hind legs went off like a chainsaw and the claws slashed through my knuckle. I got my rabbit and humanely dispatched it, but I also had a relatively minor scratch which turned badly septic and took months to heal.

Clean kill of birds

Birds are a different matter. An accurate head or neck shot to any bird (though it's a tiny target) will bring instant dispatch. A shot to the heart/lungs depends on species. No problem with magpies, jays, jackdaws. A .22 pellet to the heart/lung area will kill. The stress impact alone is enough to finish the bird. Not so with larger prey, however. The rook or carrion crow can at times withstand such a shot and may just flop to the ground.

A corvid, on the ground, retains all its wariness and suspicion so, again, the ten-yard rule applies. Get close, but no closer than ten yards, and finish the job. If you can't, you've got trouble. I will confess to having chased one crow for a quarter of a mile over a ploughed field to bring about its dispatch, but I did it, out of deference to my quarry.

Again, a knowledge of anatomy comes into play. The tough cartilage holding the wing to the body will absorb the impact of a pellet and injury will result. The pellet needs to penetrate, so it needs to enter under the tuck of the wing or between the shoulder blades to hit the heart/lung area.

Anyone who attempts a breast-shot at a pigeon with a sub-12 ft/lb airgun needs to first understand its anatomy. It has a solid breastbone cushioned with half an inch of pure meat: a potential pellet-stopper. A pricked pigeon can soar for a mile before dropping, as many shotgunners can testify. Go for the head/neck shot if possible, or a side/back shot above the breastbone. A pellet close to the tuck of the wing will stop the heart, even at sub 12ft/lb, if shot within 25 yards. If you do make a mistake, you have two options once the bird has grounded close to you. Again, the ten yard rule as with crows, but aim for the head or neck. The pigeon is less reactive than a corvid though, so when injured will often let you approach. In which case, manual dispatch is swiftest. A simple twist of the neck.

Heart/lung shots for grey squirrel

Perhaps the one airgun quarry you don't want to make a mistake with is the grey squirrel. This is one species where I will often opt for the heart/lung shot. I carry out lots of squirrel control. They have heads like walnuts - they can head-butt low power pellets, whereas the engine room shot is usually terminal. The way squirrels present themselves often gives the opportunity for the heart/lung shots anyway.

If a grey squirrel hits the ground injured, don't treat it like a rabbit. These vermin have a bite like a rat, to which many dogs can testify. Don't attempt to handle it. Get to ten yards and shoot it again. My lurcher learned long ago how to avoid the toothy end of a grey squirrel. And there's a tip. If you're serious about squirrel (or rat) control take a dog. What you don't finish, your dog will. In a fraction of the time it would take you to reach it. Please bear in mind the Hunting Act though. Make sure your dog reads it thoroughly.

Finally, a point to note. Often, dispatch of injured quarry involves being up close and personal. Death at close quarters is no different to death at long range. If you can't handle that, you have no moral right to hunt vermin. Respect your quarry and respect your sport.

Bunny, bangers and beans

A variation to my On Patrol Casserole described earlier and one which the kids will love. It also allows the Philistines around the table to pick out the rabbit if they must and enjoy the sausages instead. This is best served thick, so don't over-do the water. As far as the kids are concerned, this is packed with flavour and protein. They'll enjoy helping you make it, too, which is the first step to getting them to appreciate nature's larder.

Recipe

Two rabbits, stripped to prime cubed meat
6 or 8 thick pork sausages
Packet of sausage casserole mix
1 tin of chopped tomatoes
1 tin baked beans
A dozen button mushrooms, sliced
One large onion, chopped
A sprinkle of Worcestershire sauce
Quarter pint of water (added if needed)

Cooking and Serving

Brown the sausages under the grill first then chop them into sections. Shallow fry the rabbit to seal, then throw the whole lot into a casserole dish. Add half the water. Cook on 180 degrees for two hours to tenderise the rabbit. After an hour, add the tin of baked beans and add water if necessary. Keep it juicy, but thick. This dish is best served over a bed of Yorkshire pud and mashed potatoes. Add some sliced runner beans, dripping in butter, to the side for colour. A simple and delicious way to serve rabbit. If the kids enjoy it, tell them you won't ever make it again unless they wash up !

Bunny, bangers and beans

Acknowledgements

No man is an island, they say, but when it comes to shooting and hunting, I am fiercely isolated. Two's a crowd and three's a riot, in my eyes, with due respect to Dylan, my faithful lurcher. Yet even he can't cross onto my island unless the tide's right, by me.

I couldn't have persisted with many thousands of words and hundreds of photos unless there were someone to read and appreciate them. This book is a thank-you to all those magazine editors, fellow contributors and readers who keep our country sports press alive.

To James Marchington (*Sporting Shooter*) who led me to Nigel Allen (then with *Airgunner*), I thank you, sir. To Nigel himself, who not only encouraged my writing but taught me how to present articles and polished up my photography, I am eternally grateful. To Charlie Jacoby, Peter Carr and Wes Stanton at *Sporting Rifle*, Laoni Weeks and Tracey Allen at *Countryman's Weekly* and Camilla Clark and Alastair Balmain at *Shooting Times:* thanks for using me and keep up the good work please! The air gun fraternity depends on your publication of copy such as mine!

To Terry Doe and Matt Clark at Archant (*Airgunner* and *Airgun World*). To

Dave Nicholson and Dave Bontoft at Hull Cartridge who have given trojan support. To Chris Youngman, Pellpax, Uttings, and many others, thanks for your superb customer seervice and help with prompt supply when needed. To those who failed, read it and weep. Thanks to my fellow scribes Mat Manning and Jim Tyler, who share my crazy obsession with documenting the hunt.

A hunter, without permission to shoot on someone's land, is like a sailor without a sea. I would particularly like to thank Oliver & Hannah Arnold, Edward & Victoria Jones, Lady Anne Prince-Smith, Jimmy Hall and Trevor Moy, all of whom own a piece of Norfolk and allow me to play in their 'back gardens'.

I hope I've made a small difference, especially where crops and songbirds are concerned. I hope this book is a legacy for your children, that they understand how important it is to have the freedom to walk the fields and woods, with a gun and a dog, in the interests of conservation. This book is about your land and I have been privileged to walk it.

To young Sam, my son, torn from the computer so many times and forced into the wet and cold at Dad's behest, so that he could learn country ways. Have you? Will you, when I'm gone? I sincerely hope so.

Last, but certainly not least, my dear Cheryl. My wife, my best friend, my shooting widow and my inspiration. I love you, babe!

How does she put up with me?

A hunter's prayer

If reincarnation is a truth, please let me come back as a fox, so that I may still hunt my rabbits on a summer's evening, that I may still lie in the shade of a beech to watch the sunset and that I may still make my way through the world with not just a little bit of cunning but also an eye for mischief.

Ian Barnett, Norfolk

Index

Useful airgun addresses

Suppliers

These are suppliers who I can only say have given me good service over the years.

Air Arms (rifles, pellets)   www.air-arms.co.uk
Bushwear (supplies/clothing)   www.bushwear.co.uk   0845 226 0469
BSA (rifles, scopes)   www.bsaguns.co.uk
Deben Industries (supplies, clothing)   www.deben.com   01394 387762
Hull Cartridge Co (Weihrauch guns)   www.hullcartridge.co.uk
Pellpax (rifles, supplies, pellets)   www.pellpax.co.uk   01263 514848
JS Ramsbottom (supplies, scopes)   www.jsramsbottom.com
Michael Tawn (supplies)   www.tawnadoairguns.com   01945 420770
Sportsman Gun Centre (supplies)   www.sportsmanguncentre.com
The Airgun Centre (rifles)   www.theairguncentre.com   01268 780730
Uttings (supplies, clothing)   www.uttings.co.uk   01603 619811
Webley (rifles)   www.webley.co.uk   01902 722144
Youngmans Guns (supplies)   www.youngmans.com   01493 859814

Shooting organisations, insurers and legal advice

No sensible shooter will venture out without liability insurance. The organisations below will insure you for a pittance, give legal advice, help with Firearms Certification, general shooting advice and you get a few magazines a year thrown in too. If you find yourself on the wrong side of the law – call Clive! I've never had to, but I've followed his articles in *Countryman's Weekly* and he has a wealth of experience.

BASC – British Association for Shooting & Conservation
     www.basc.org.uk   01244 573030
CA – Countryside Alliance
     www.countryside-alliance.org.uk   020 7840 9300
NGO – National Gamekeepers' Organisation
     www.nationalgamekeepers.org.uk 01833 660869
Clive Rees – Hunting lawyer
     clive_rees@yahoo.co.uk   07969 378750

Shooting Press (magazines)

There's rarely such thing as a 'bad' read when it comes to shooting. Keeping up-to-date with guns, kit and methods is valuable.

Airgun Shooter, Sporting Rifle
www.blazepublishing.co.uk 01926 339808

Airgunner, Airgun World, Sporting Shooter
www.airgunshooting.co.uk 01858 438840

The Countryman's Weekly
www.countrymansweekly.com 01752 762984

Shooting Times, Sporting Gun
www.magazinesdirect.co.uk 0845 6767778

Internet resources

There are numerous web forums where you can interact with other shooters from the comfort of your home. They can be informative: you can get help with problems and they can be humourous. Be warned, though, they can also be sparky, inhabited by imbeciles and carry poor advice too. The forums below are the ones I haven't yet been banned from!

www.airarmsownersclub.com
www.airgunbbs.com
www.airgunforum.net
www.airgununiverse.co.uk
www.thehuntinglife.com
www.verminhunter.com

Further reading from Merlin Unwin Books

Private Thoughts from a Small Shoot
Laurence Catlow £17.99

That Strange Alchemy
Pheasants, trout and a middle-aged man
Laurence Catlow £17.99

Wild Duck - and their pursuit
Douglas Butler £20

Rough Shooting in Ireland
Douglas Butler £20

Vintage Guns for the Modern Shot
Diggory Hadoke £30

The Poacher's Handbook
Ian Niall £14.95

The Poacher's Cookbook
Prue Coats £11.99

Advice from a Gamekeeper
John Cowan £20

The Shootingman's Bedside Book
by BB £18.95

The Countryman's Bedside Book
by BB £18.95

The Best of BB
An anthology £18.95

Apley Hall
The golden years of a sporting estate
Norman Sharpe £12

The Hare
Jill Mason £20

The Otter
James Williams £20

Hunting in the Lake District
Seán Frain £14.99

Willie Irving
Terrierman, Huntsman and Lakelander
Sean Frain £17.99

Over the Farmer's Gate
Roger Evans £12

The Fisherman's Bedside Book
by BB £18.95

The Manual of a Traditional Bacon Curer
Maynard Davies £25

Mushrooming Without Fear
Alexander Schwab £14.99

These books can be ordered from all good bookshops, or from our website:
www.merlinunwin.co.uk